SDL Game Development

Discover how to leverage the power of SDL 2.0 to create awesome games in C++

Shaun Ross Mitchell

[PACKT] PUBLISHING

BIRMINGHAM - MUMBAI

SDL Game Development

Copyright © 2013 Packt Publishing

All rights reserved. No part of this book may be reproduced, stored in a retrieval system, or transmitted in any form or by any means, without the prior written permission of the publisher, except in the case of brief quotations embedded in critical articles or reviews.

Every effort has been made in the preparation of this book to ensure the accuracy of the information presented. However, the information contained in this book is sold without warranty, either express or implied. Neither the author, nor Packt Publishing, and its dealers and distributors will be held liable for any damages caused or alleged to be caused directly or indirectly by this book.

Packt Publishing has endeavored to provide trademark information about all of the companies and products mentioned in this book by the appropriate use of capitals. However, Packt Publishing cannot guarantee the accuracy of this information.

First published: June 2013

Production Reference: 1170613

Published by Packt Publishing Ltd.
Livery Place
35 Livery Street
Birmingham B3 2PB, UK.

ISBN 978-1-84969-682-1

www.packtpub.com

Cover Image by Shaun Mitchell (shaunmitchell84@googlemail.com)

Credits

Author
Shaun Ross Mitchell

Reviewers
Luka Horvat
Mårten Möller

Acquisition Editor
Edward Gordon

Lead Technical Editor
Savio Jose
Chalini Snega Victor

Technical Editors
Jeeten Handu
Kaustubh S. Mayekar
Anita Nayak

Project Coordinator
Hardik Patel

Proofreader
Bernadette Watkins

Indexer
Rekha Nair

Graphics
Ronak Dhruv

Production Coordinator
Prachali Bhiwandkar

Cover Work
Prachali Bhiwandkar

About the Author

Shaun Mitchell is a developer at a high profile online gaming company. He holds a BSc in Game Programming and Development from Qantm College / SAE Institute London. Shaun is also a moderator and active member of the <dream.in.code> programming community.

> I would like to thank Jason Colman, my university lecturer, whose knowledge and insight into C++ and game programming has been the foundation of my skillset.
>
> I would also like to thank the <dream.in.code> community for the interesting discussions and topics to hone my skills with.
>
> Thank you to John Bayly for the background image on the front cover.
>
> Many thanks to my family for their continued support and importantly, a huge thank you to my girlfriend, Emma, who tirelessly proofread my chapters while also keeping me running on a generous amount of caffeine.

About the Reviewers

Luka Horvat is an enthusiastic software and game developer who got fascinated by computer science in his early years. He chose to study his passion while working on many different projects and technologies. Throughout the years he gained a lot of knowledge and experience, and he wanted to share that with others. He is proficient in many different programming languages, with C++ as his main one; and is passionate about game development. So he started teaching it and currently manages different courses for in this area. He continues to pursue his career in computer science by working on a wide variety of projects and sharing them with others.

> I would like to thank my friends and family who helped me produce this book.

Mårten Möller is an independent game developer who has previously worked at Imperial Game Studios.

> I would like to thank my family and friends. All of you are amazing.

www.PacktPub.com

Support files, eBooks, discount offers and more

You might want to visit www.PacktPub.com for support files and downloads related to your book.

Did you know that Packt offers eBook versions of every book published, with PDF and ePub files available? You can upgrade to the eBook version at www.PacktPub.com and as a print book customer, you are entitled to a discount on the eBook copy. Get in touch with us at service@packtpub.com for more details.

At www.PacktPub.com, you can also read a collection of free technical articles, sign up for a range of free newsletters and receive exclusive discounts and offers on Packt books and eBooks.

PACKTLIB

http://PacktLib.PacktPub.com

Do you need instant solutions to your IT questions? PacktLib is Packt's online digital book library. Here, you can access, read and search across Packt's entire library of books.

Why Subscribe?

- Fully searchable across every book published by Packt
- Copy and paste, print and bookmark content
- On demand and accessible via web browser

Free Access for Packt account holders

If you have an account with Packt at www.PacktPub.com, you can use this to access PacktLib today and view nine entirely free books. Simply use your login credentials for immediate access.

In memory of my Mum.
You always believed in me.
I miss you everyday.

Table of Contents

Preface	**1**
Chapter 1: Getting Started with SDL	**5**
Why use SDL?	**6**
What is new in SDL 2.0?	6
Migrating SDL 1.2 extensions	7
Setting up SDL in Visual C++ Express 2010	**8**
Using Mercurial to get SDL 2.0 on Windows	8
Cloning and building the latest SDL 2.0 repository	8
I have the library; now what?	10
Hello SDL	**13**
An overview of Hello SDL	14
SDL initialization flags	16
SDL renderer flags	17
What makes up a game	**17**
Breaking up the Hello SDL code	18
What does this code do?	20
The Game class	**21**
Fullscreen SDL	26
Summary	**28**
Chapter 2: Drawing in SDL	**29**
Basic SDL drawing	**29**
Getting some images	29
Creating an SDL texture	30
Source and destination rectangles	**32**
Animating a sprite sheet	35
Flipping images	37
Installing SDL_image	**38**
Using SDL_image	40

Tying it into the framework	**42**
Creating the texture manager	42
Using texture manager as a singleton	46
Summary	**47**
Chapter 3: Working with Game Objects	**49**
Using inheritance	49
Implementing polymorphism	55
Using abstract base classes	60
Should we always use inheritance?	61
Could the same thing be achieved with a simpler solution?	61
Derived classes should model the "is a" relationship	61
Possible performance penalties	62
Putting it all together	62
Summary	**67**
Chapter 4: Exploring Movement and Input Handling	**69**
Setting up game objects for movement	**70**
What is a vector?	70
Some common operations	72
Addition of two vectors	72
Multiply by a scalar number	73
Subtraction of two vectors	73
Divide by a scalar number	74
Normalizing a vector	74
Adding the Vector2D class	75
Adding velocity	76
Adding acceleration	77
Creating fixed frames per second	**77**
Input handling	**79**
Creating our input handler class	79
Handling joystick/gamepad input	80
SDL joystick events	80
Initializing joysticks	81
Listening for and handling axis movement	84
Dealing with joystick button input	91
Handling mouse events	93
Using mouse button events	93
Handling mouse motion events	95
Implementing keyboard input	96
Wrapping things up	98
Summary	**100**

Chapter 5: Handling Game States — 101
- **A simple way for switching states** — 101
- **Implementing finite state machines** — 103
  - A base class for game states — 103
  - Implementing FSM — 106
- **Implementing menu states** — 110
  - Function pointers and callback functions — 114
  - Implementing the temporary play state — 117
  - Pausing the game — 120
  - Creating the game over state — 123
- **Summary** — 130

Chapter 6: Data-driven Design — 131
- **Loading XML files** — 131
  - Basic XML structure — 132
- **Implementing Object Factories** — 134
  - Using Distributed Factories — 135
- **Fitting the factory into the framework** — 138
- **Parsing states from an XML file** — 140
- **Loading the menu state from an XML file** — 147
- **Loading other states from an XML file** — 150
  - Loading the play state — 150
  - Loading the pause state — 152
  - Loading the game over state — 153
- **Summary** — 155

Chapter 7: Creating and Displaying Tile Maps — 157
- **What is a tile map?** — 158
- **Getting familiar with the Tiled application** — 160
- **Parsing and drawing a tile map** — 165
  - Creating the TileLayer class — 167
  - Creating the LevelParser class — 168
  - Parsing tilesets — 170
  - Parsing a tile layer — 171
  - Drawing the map — 175
- **Scrolling a tile map** — 180
- **Parsing object layers** — 182
  - Developing the ObjectLayer class — 184
- **Summary** — 189

Table of Contents

Chapter 8: Creating Alien Attack — 191
Using the SDL_mixer extension for sound — 193
Creating the SoundManager class — 193
Setting up the basic game objects — 196
GameObject revamped — 196
SDLGameObject is now ShooterObject — 199
Player inherits from ShooterObject — 200
Lots of enemy types — 204
Adding a scrolling background — 205
Handling bullets — 207
Two types of bullets — 207
The BulletHandler class — 209
Dealing with collisions — 211
Creating a CollisionManager class — 214
Possible improvements — 216
Summary — 216

Chapter 9: Creating Conan the Caveman — 217
Setting up the basic game objects — 218
No more bullets or bullet collisions — 218
Game objects and map collisions — 219
ShooterObject is now PlatformerObject — 219
The Camera class — 222
Camera-controlled map — 224
The Player class — 225
Possible additions — 231
Summary — 231

Index — 233

Preface

Creating games in C++ is a complicated process requiring a lot of time and dedication to achieve results. A good foundation of reusable classes can speed up development time and allow focus to be on creating a great game rather than struggling with low-level code. This book aims to show an approach to creating a reusable framework that could be used for any game, whether 2D or 3D.

What this book covers

Chapter 1, Getting started with SDL, covers setting up SDL in Visual C++ 2010 express and then moves onto the basics of SDL including creating a window and listening for quit events.

Chapter 2, Drawing in SDL, covers the development of some core drawing classes to help simplify SDL rendering. The `SDL_image` extension is also introduced to allow the loading of a variety of different image file types.

Chapter 3, Working with Game Objects, gives a basic introduction to inheritance and polymorphism along with the development of a reusable `GameObject` class that will be used throughout the rest of the book.

Chapter 4, Exploring Movement and Input Handling, gives a detailed look at handling events in SDL. Joystick, keyboard, and mouse input are all covered with the development of reusable classes.

Chapter 5, Handling Game States, covers the design and implementation of a finite state machine to manage game states. Implementing and moving between different states is covered in detail.

Chapter 6, Data-driven Design, covers the use of TinyXML to load states. A class to parse states is developed along with examples for different states.

Preface

Chapter 7, Creating and Displaying Tile Maps, brings together everything from the previous chapters to allow the creation of levels using the Tiled map editor. A level parsing class is created to load maps from an XML file.

Chapter 8, Creating Alien Attack, covers the creation of a 2D side scrolling shooter, utilizing everything learned in the previous chapters.

Chapter 9, Creating Conan the Caveman, covers the creation of a second game, altering the code from Alien Attack, showing that the framework is flexible enough to be used for any 2D game genre.

What you need for this book

To use this book you will need the following software:

- Visual C++ 2010 Express
- Tiled map editor
- TinyXML
- zlib library

Who this book is for

This book is aimed at beginner/intermediate C++ programmers who want to take their existing skills and apply them to creating games in C++. This is not a beginner's book and you are expected to know the basics of C++, including inheritance, polymorphism, and class design.

Conventions

In this book, you will find a number of styles of text that distinguish between different kinds of information. Here are some examples of these styles, and an explanation of their meaning.

Code words in text are shown as follows: "We can include other contexts through the use of the `include` directive."

A block of code is set as follows:

```
void Player::update()
{
  m_currentFrame = int(((SDL_GetTicks() / 100) % 6));
```

```
    m_acceleration.setX(1);

    SDLGameObject::update();
}
```

New terms and **important words** are shown in bold. Words that you see on the screen, in menus or dialog boxes for example, appear in the text like this: "Right-click on the project and choose **Build**.".

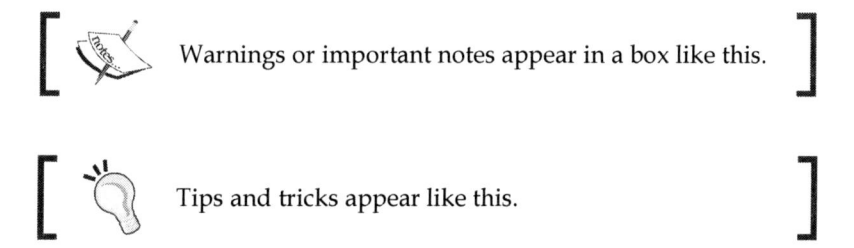

> Warnings or important notes appear in a box like this.

> Tips and tricks appear like this.

Reader feedback

Feedback from our readers is always welcome. Let us know what you think about this book—what you liked or may have disliked. Reader feedback is important for us to develop titles that you really get the most out of.

To send us general feedback, simply send an e-mail to feedback@packtpub.com, and mention the book title via the subject of your message.

If there is a topic that you have expertise in and you are interested in either writing or contributing to a book, see our author guide on www.packtpub.com/authors.

Customer support

Now that you are the proud owner of a Packt book, we have a number of things to help you to get the most from your purchase.

Downloading the example code

You can download the example code files for all Packt books you have purchased from your account at http://www.packtpub.com. If you purchased this book elsewhere, you can visit http://www.packtpub.com/support and register to have the files e-mailed directly to you.

Errata

Although we have taken every care to ensure the accuracy of our content, mistakes do happen. If you find a mistake in one of our books—maybe a mistake in the text or the code—we would be grateful if you would report this to us. By doing so, you can save other readers from frustration and help us improve subsequent versions of this book. If you find any errata, please report them by visiting http://www.packtpub.com/submit-errata, selecting your book, clicking on the **erratasubmissionform** link, and entering the details of your errata. Once your errata are verified, your submission will be accepted and the errata will be uploaded on our website, or added to any list of existing errata, under the Errata section of that title. Any existing errata can be viewed by selecting your title from http://www.packtpub.com/support.

Piracy

Piracy of copyright material on the Internet is an ongoing problem across all media. At Packt, we take the protection of our copyright and licenses very seriously. If you come across any illegal copies of our works, in any form, on the Internet, please provide us with the location address or website name immediately so that we can pursue a remedy.

Please contact us at copyright@packtpub.com with a link to the suspected pirated material.

We appreciate your help in protecting our authors, and our ability to bring you valuable content.

Questions

You can contact us at questions@packtpub.com if you are having a problem with any aspect of the book, and we will do our best to address it.

1
Getting Started with SDL

Simple DirectMedia Layer (SDL) is a cross-platform multimedia library created by Sam Oscar Latinga. It provides low-level access to input (via mouse, keyboard, and gamepads/joysticks), 3D hardware, and the 2D video frame buffer. SDL is written in the C programming language, yet has native support for C++. The library also has bindings for several other languages such as Pascal, Objective-C, Python, Ruby, and Java; a full list of supported languages is available at http://www.libsdl.org/languages.php.

SDL has been used in many commercial games including World of Goo, Neverwinter Nights, and Second Life. It is also used in emulators such as ZSNES, Mupen64, and VisualBoyAdvance. Some popular games ported to Linux platforms such as Quake 4, Soldier of Fortune, and Civilization: Call to Power utilize SDL in some form.

SDL is not just used for games. It is useful for all manner of applications. If your software needs access to graphics and input, chances are that SDL will be a great help. The SDL official website has a list of applications that have been created using the library (http://www.libsdl.org/applications.php).

In this chapter we will cover the following:

- Getting the latest SDL build from the Mercurial repository
- Building and setting up SDL in Visual C++ 2010 Express
- Creating a window with SDL
- Implementing a basic game class

Why use SDL?

Each platform has its own way of creating and displaying windows and graphics, handling user input, and accessing any low-level hardware; each one with its own intricacies and syntax. SDL provides a uniform way of accessing these platform-specific features. This uniformity leads to more time spent tweaking your game rather than worrying about how a specific platform allows you to render or get user input, and so on. Game programming can be quite difficult, and having a library such as SDL can get your game up and running relatively quickly.

The ability to write a game on Windows and then go on to compile it on OSX or Linux with little to no changes in the code is extremely powerful and perfect for developers who want to target as many platforms as possible; SDL makes this kind of cross-platform development a breeze. While SDL is extremely effective for cross-platform development, it is also an excellent choice for creating a game with just one platform in mind, due to its ease of use and abundance of features.

SDL has a large user base and is being actively updated and maintained. There is also a responsive community along with a helpful mailing list. Documentation for SDL 2.0 is up-to-date and constantly maintained. Visiting the SDL website, libsdl.org, offers up lots of articles and information with links to the documentation, mailing list, and forums.

Overall, SDL offers a great place to start with game development, allowing you to focus on the game itself and ignore which platform you are developing for, until it is completely necessary. Now, with SDL 2.0 and the new features it brings to the table, SDL has become an even more capable library for game development using C++.

> The best way to find out what you can do with SDL and its various functions is to use the documentation found at http://wiki.libsdl.org/moin.cgi/CategoryAPI. There you can see a list of all of SDL 2.0's functions along with various code examples.

What is new in SDL 2.0?

The latest version of SDL and SDL 2.0, which we will be covering in this book, is still in development. It adds many new features to the existing SDL 1.2 framework. The SDL 2.0 Roadmap (wiki.libsdl.org/moin.cgi/Roadmap) lists these features as:

- A 3D accelerated, texture-based rendering API
- Hardware-accelerated 2D graphics
- Support for render targets

- Multiple window support
- API support for clipboard access
- Multiple input device support
- Support for 7.1 audio
- Multiple audio device support
- Force-feedback API for joysticks
- Horizontal mouse wheel support
- Multitouch input API support
- Audio capture support
- Improvements to multithreading

While not all of these will be used in our game-programming adventures, some of them are invaluable and make SDL an even better framework to use to develop games. We will be taking advantage of the new hardware-accelerated 2D graphics to make sure our games have excellent performance.

Migrating SDL 1.2 extensions

SDL has separate extensions that can be used to add new capabilities to the library. The reason these extensions are not included in the first place is to keep SDL as lightweight as possible, with the extensions serving to add functionality only when necessary. The next table shows some useful extensions along with their purpose. These extensions have been updated from their SDL1.2/3 Versions to support SDL 2.0, and this book will cover cloning and building them from their respective repositories as and when they are needed.

Name	Description
SDL_image	This is an image file loading library with support for BMP, GIF, PNG, TGA, PCX, and among others.
SDL_net	This is a cross-platform networking library.
SDL_mixer	This is an audio mixer library. It has support for MP3, MIDI, and OGG.
SDL_ttf	This is a library supporting the use of TrueType fonts in SDL applications.
SDL_rtf	This is a library to support the rendering of the **Rich Text Format** (**RTF**).

Setting up SDL in Visual C++ Express 2010

This book will cover setting up SDL 2.0 in Microsoft's Visual C++ Express 2010 IDE. This IDE was chosen as it is available for free online, and is a widely used development environment within the games industry. The application is available at https://www.microsoft.com/visualstudio/en-gb/express. Once the IDE has been installed we can go ahead and download SDL 2.0. If you are not using Windows to develop games, then these instructions can be altered to suit your IDE of choice using its specific steps to link libraries and include files.

SDL 2.0 is still in development so there are no official releases as yet. The library can be retrieved in two different ways:

- One is to download the under-construction snapshot; you can then link against this to build your games (the quickest option)
- The second option is to clone the latest source using mercurial-distributed source control and build it from scratch (a good option to keep up with the latest developments of the library)

Both of these options are available at http://www.libsdl.org/hg.php.

Building SDL 2.0 on Windows also requires the latest DirectX SDK, which is available at http://www.microsoft.com/en-gb/download/details.aspx?id=6812, so make sure this is installed first.

Using Mercurial to get SDL 2.0 on Windows

Getting SDL 2.0 directly from the constantly updated repository is the best way of making sure you have the latest build of SDL 2.0 and that you are taking advantage of any current bug fixes. To download and build the latest version of SDL 2.0 on Windows, we must first install a mercurial source control client so that we can mirror the latest source code and build from it. There are various command-line tools and GUIs available for use with mercurial. We will use TortoiseHg, a free and user-friendly mercurial application; it is available at tortoisehg.bitbucket.org. Once the application is installed, we can go ahead and grab the latest build.

Cloning and building the latest SDL 2.0 repository

Cloning and building the latest version of SDL directly from the repository is relatively straightforward when following these steps:

1. Open up the **TortoiseHg Workbench** window.

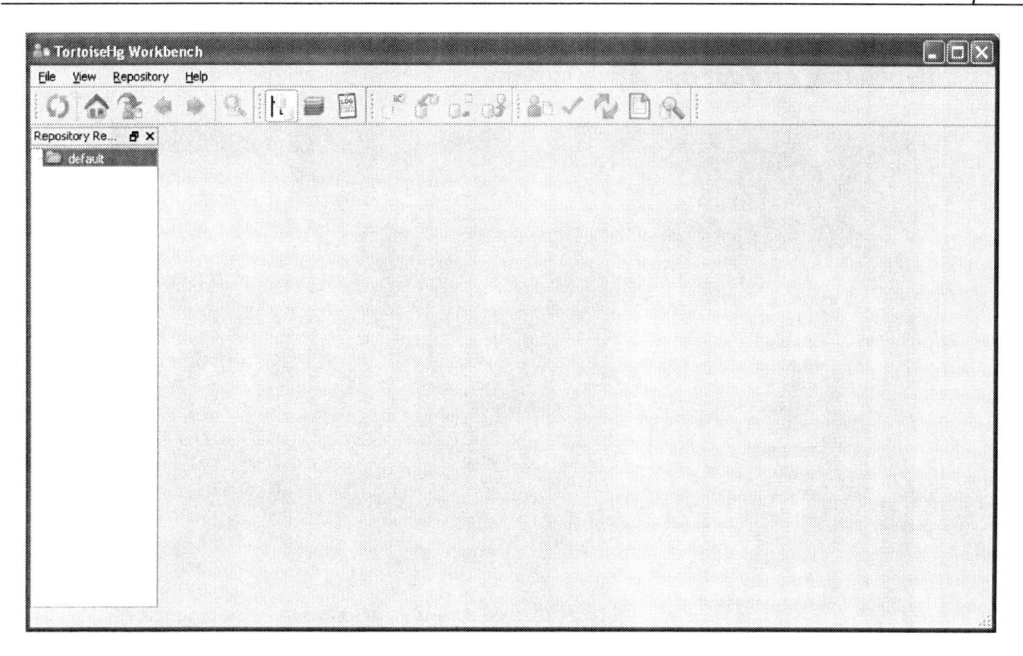

2. Pressing *Ctrl + Shift + N* will open the clone dialog box.
3. Input the source of the repository; in this case it is listed on the SDL 2.0 website as `http://hg.libsdl.org/SDL`.
4. Input or browse to choose a destination for the cloned repository—this book will assume that `C:\SDL2` is set as the location.
5. Click on **Clone** and allow the repository to copy to the chosen destination.
6. Within the `C:\SDL2` directory there will be a `VisualC` folder; inside the folder there is a Visual C++ 2010 solution, which we have to open with Visual C++ Express 2010.
7. Visual C++ Express will throw up a few errors about solution folders not being supported in the express version, but they can be safely ignored without affecting our ability to build the library.

Getting Started with SDL

8. Change the current build configuration to release and also choose 32 or 64 bit depending on your operating system.

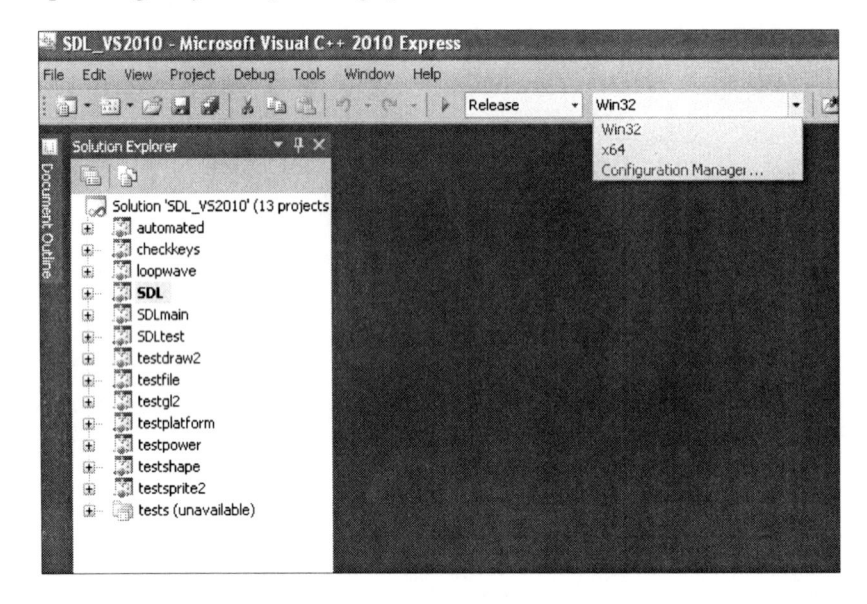

9. Right-click on the project named **SDL** listed in the **Solution Explorer** list and choose **Build**.
10. We now have a build of the SDL 2.0 library to use. It will be located at `C:\SDL2\VisualC\SDL\Win32(or x64)\Release\SDL.lib`.
11. We also need to build the SDL main library file, so choose it within the **Solution Explorer** list and build it. This file will build to `C:\SDL2\VisualC\SDLmain\Win32(or x64)\Release\SDLmain.lib`.
12. Create a folder named `lib` in `C:\SDL2` and copy `SDL.lib` and `SDLmain.lib` into this newly created folder.

I have the library; now what?

Now a Visual C++ 2010 project can be created and linked with the SDL library. Here are the steps involved:

1. Create a new empty project in Visual C++ express and give it a name, such as `SDL-game`.
2. Once created, right-click on the project in the **Solution Explorer** list and choose **Properties**.

Chapter 1

3. Change the configuration drop-down list to **All Configurations**.
4. Under **VC++ Directories**, click on **Include Directories**. A small arrow will allow a drop-down menu; click on **<Edit...>**.

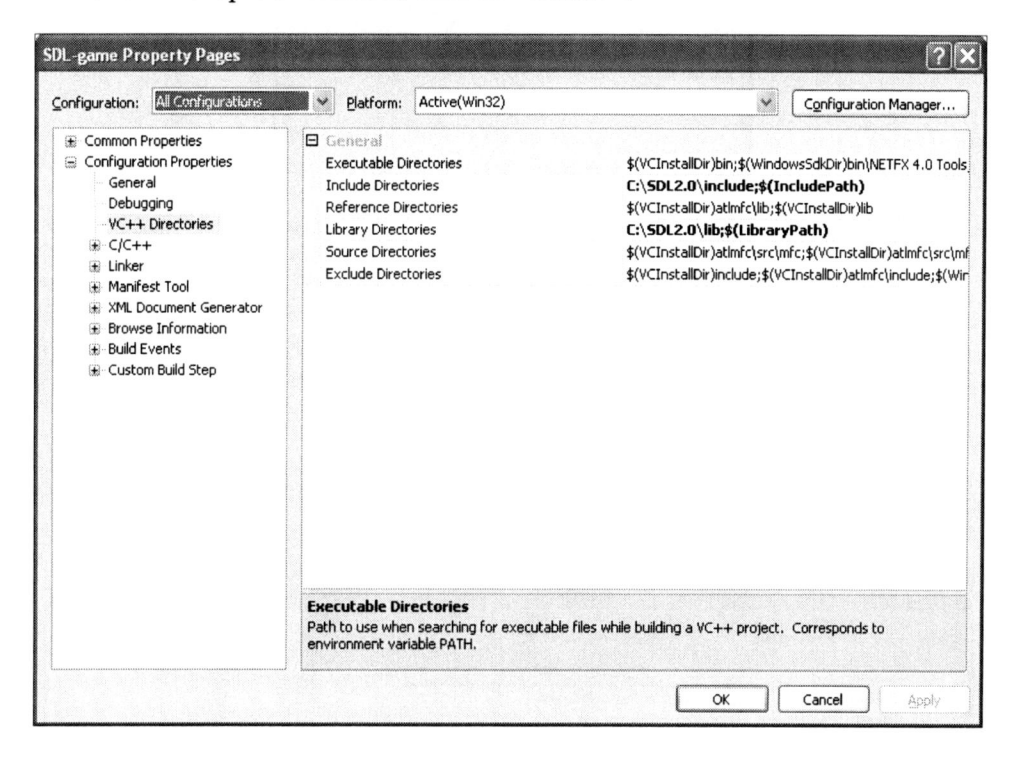

5. Double-click inside the box to create a new location. You can type or browse to `C:\SDL2.0\include` and click on **OK**.
6. Next, do the same thing under library directories, this time passing in your created `lib` folder (`C:\SDL2\lib`).

Getting Started with SDL

7. Next, navigate to the **Linker** heading; inside the heading there will be an **Input** choice. Inside **Additional Dependencies** type `SDL.lib SDLmain.lib`:

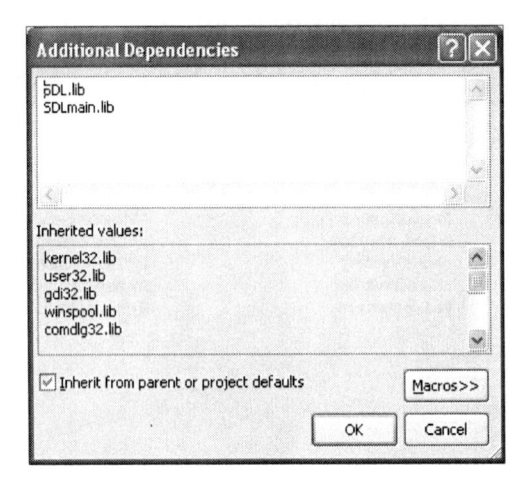

8. Navigate to the **System** heading and set the **SubSystem** heading to **Windows(/SUBSYSTEM:WINDOWS)**.

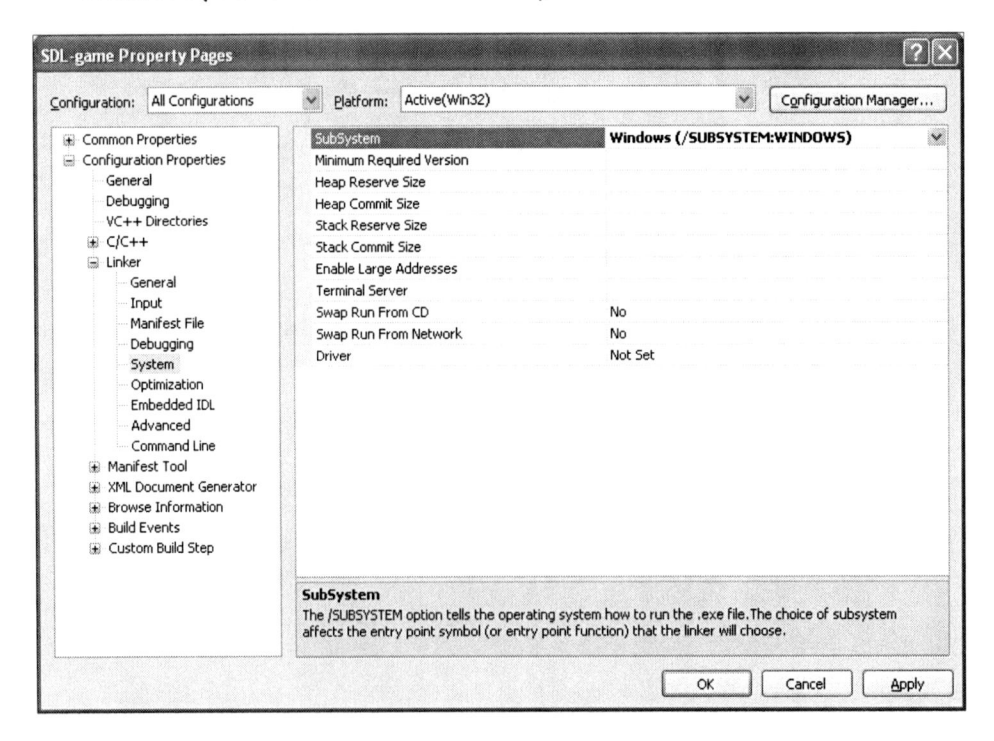

9. Click on **OK** and we are done.

[12]

Hello SDL

We now have an empty project, which links to the SDL library, so it is time to start our SDL development. Click on **Source Files** and use the keyboard shortcut *Ctrl + Shift + A* to add a new item. Create a C++ file called `main.cpp`. After creating this file, copy the following code into the source file:

```cpp
#include<SDL.h>

SDL_Window* g_pWindow = 0;
SDL_Renderer* g_pRenderer = 0;

int main(int argc, char* args[])
{
  // initialize SDL
  if(SDL_Init(SDL_INIT_EVERYTHING) >= 0)
  {
    // if succeeded create our window
    g_pWindow = SDL_CreateWindow("Chapter 1: Setting up SDL",
      SDL_WINDOWPOS_CENTERED, SDL_WINDOWPOS_CENTERED,
      640, 480,
      SDL_WINDOW_SHOWN);

    // if the window creation succeeded create our renderer
    if(g_pWindow != 0)
    {
      g_pRenderer = SDL_CreateRenderer(g_pWindow, -1, 0);
    }
  }
  else
  {
    return 1; // sdl could not initialize
  }

  // everything succeeded lets draw the window

  // set to black // This function expects Red, Green, Blue and
  //  Alpha as color values
  SDL_SetRenderDrawColor(g_pRenderer, 0, 0, 0, 255);

  // clear the window to black
  SDL_RenderClear(g_pRenderer);

  // show the window
```

```
    SDL_RenderPresent(g_pRenderer);

    // set a delay before quitting
    SDL_Delay(5000);

    // clean up SDL
    SDL_Quit();

    return 0;
}
```

We can now attempt to build our first SDL application. Right-click on the project and choose **Build**. There will be an error about the `SDL.dll` file not being found:

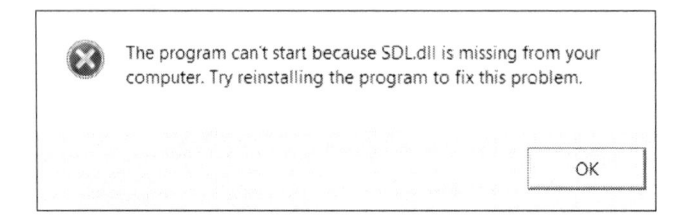

The attempted build should have created a `Debug` or `Release` folder within the project directory (usually located in your `Documents` folder under visual studio and projects). This folder contains the `.exe` file from our attempted build; we need to add the `SDL.dll` file to this folder. The `SDL.dll` file is located at `C:\SDL2\VisualC\SDL\Win32` (or `x64`) `\Release\SDL.dll` 1). When you want to distribute your game to another computer, you will have to share this file as well as the executable. After you have added the `SDL.dll` file to the executable folder, the project will now compile and show an SDL window; wait for 5 seconds and then close.

An overview of Hello SDL

Let's go through the `Hello SDL` code:

1. First, we included the `SDL.h` header file so that we have access to all of SDL's functions:

   `#include<SDL.h>`

2. The next step is to create some global variables. One is a pointer to an `SDL_Window` function, which will be set using the `SDL_CreateWindow` function. The second is a pointer to an `SDL_Renderer` object; set using the `SDL_CreateRenderer` function:

   ```
   SDL_Window* g_pWindow = 0;
   SDL_Renderer* g_pRenderer = 0;
   ```

Chapter 1

3. We can now initialize SDL. This example initializes all of SDL's subsystems using the `SDL_INIT_EVERYTHING` flag, but this does not always have to be the case (see SDL initialization flags):

   ```
   int main(int argc, char* argv[])
   {
     // initialize SDL
     if(SDL_Init(SDL_INIT_EVERYTHING) >= 0)
       {
   ```

4. If the SDL initialization was successful, we can create the pointer to our window. `SDL_CreateWindow` returns a pointer to a window matching the passed parameters. The parameters are the window title, *x* position of the window, *y* position of the window, width, height, and any required `SDL_flags` (we will cover these later in the chapter). `SDL_WINDOWPOS_CENTERED` will center our window relative to the screen:

   ```
   // if succeeded create our window
   g_pWindow = SDL_CreateWindow("Chapter 1: Setting up SDL", SDL_WINDOWPOS_CENTERED, SDL_WINDOWPOS_CENTERED, 640, 480, SDL_WINDOW_SHOWN);
   ```

5. We can now check whether the window creation was successful, and if so, move on to set the pointer to our renderer, passing the window we want the renderer to use as a parameter; in our case, it is the newly created `g_pWindow` pointer. The second parameter passed is the index of the rendering driver to initialize; in this case, we use `-1` to use the first capable driver. The final parameter is `SDL_RendererFlag` (see SDL renderer flags):

   ```
   // if the window creation succeeded create our renderer
   if(g_pWindow != 0)
   {
     g_pRenderer = SDL_CreateRenderer(g_pWindow, -1, 0);
   }
   else
   {
     return 1; // sdl could not initialize
   }
   ```

6. If everything was successful, we can now create and show our window:

   ```
   // everything succeeded lets draw the window

     // set to black
   SDL_SetRenderDrawColor(g_pRenderer, 0, 0, 0, 255);
   ```

```
    // clear the window to black
SDL_RenderClear(g_pRenderer);

    // show the window
SDL_RenderPresent(g_pRenderer);

    // set a delay before quitting
SDL_Delay(5000);

    // clean up SDL
SDL_Quit();
```

SDL initialization flags

Event handling, file I/O, and threading subsystems are all initialized by default in SDL. Other subsystems can be initialized using the following flags:

Flag	Initialized subsystem(s)
SDL_INIT_HAPTIC	Force feedback subsystem
SDL_INIT_AUDIO	Audio subsystem
SDL_INIT_VIDEO	Video subsystem
SDL_INIT_TIMER	Timer subsystem
SDL_INIT_JOYSTICK	Joystick subsystem
SDL_INIT_EVERYTHING	All subsystems
SDL_INIT_NOPARACHUTE	Don't catch fatal signals

We can also use bitwise (|) to initialize more than one subsystem. To initialize only the audio and video subsystems, we can use a call to SDL_Init, for example:

```
SDL_Init(SDL_INIT_AUDIO | SDL_INIT_VIDEO);
```

Checking whether a subsystem has been initialized or not can be done with a call to the SDL_WasInit() function:

```
if(SDL_WasInit(SDL_INIT_VIDEO) != 0)
{
  cout << "video was initialized";
}
```

SDL renderer flags

When initializing an `SDL_Renderer` flag, we can pass in a flag to determine its behavior. The following table describes each flag's purpose:

Flag	Purpose
SDL_RENDERER_SOFTWARE	Use software rendering
SDL_RENDERER_ACCELERATED	Use hardware acceleration
SDL_RENDERER_PRESENTVSYNC	Synchronize renderer update with screen's refresh rate
SDL_RENDERER_TARGETTEXTURE	Supports render to texture

What makes up a game

Outside the design and gameplay of a game, the underlying mechanics are essentially the interaction of various subsystems such as graphics, game logic, and user input. The graphics subsystem should not know how the game logic is implemented or vice versa. We can think of the structure of a game as follows:

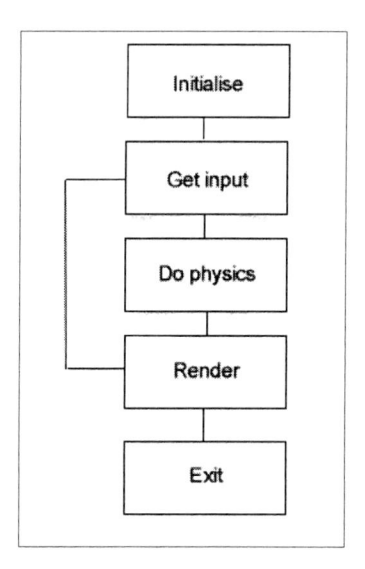

Once the game is initialized, it then goes into a loop of checking for user input, updating any values based on the game physics, before rendering to the screen. Once the user chooses to exit, the loop is broken and the game moves onto cleaning everything up and exiting. This is the basic scaffold for a game and it is what will be used in this book.

Getting Started with SDL

We will be building a reusable framework that will take all of the legwork out of creating a game in SDL 2.0. When it comes to boilerplate code and setup code, we really only want to write it once and then reuse it within new projects. The same can be done with drawing code, event handling, map loading, game states, and anything else that all games may require. We will start by breaking up the Hello SDL 2.0 example into separate parts. This will help us to start thinking about how code can be broken into reusable standalone chunks rather than packing everything into one large file.

Breaking up the Hello SDL code

We can break up the Hello SDL into separate functions:

```
bool g_bRunning = false; // this will create a loop
```

Follow these steps to break the `Hello SDL` code:

1. Create an `init` function after the two global variables that takes any necessary values as parameters and passes them to the `SDL_CreateWindow` function:

    ```
    bool init(const char* title, int xpos, int ypos, int
    height, int width, int flags)
    {
      // initialize SDL
      if(SDL_Init(SDL_INIT_EVERYTHING) >= 0)
      {
        // if succeeded create our window
        g_pWindow = SDL_CreateWindow(title, xpos, ypos,
        height, width, flags);

        // if the window creation succeeded create our
        renderer
        if(g_pWindow != 0)
        {
          g_pRenderer = SDL_CreateRenderer(g_pWindow, -1, 0);
        }
      }
      else
      {
        return false; // sdl could not initialize
      }

      return true;
    ```

```
    }

    void render()
    {
      // set to black
      SDL_SetRenderDrawColor(g_pRenderer, 0, 0, 0, 255);

      // clear the window to black
      SDL_RenderClear(g_pRenderer);

      // show the window
      SDL_RenderPresent(g_pRenderer);
    }
```

2. Our main function can now use these functions to initialize SDL:

```
    int main(int argc, char* argv[])
    {
      if(init("Chapter 1: Setting up SDL",
      SDL_WINDOWPOS_CENTERED, SDL_WINDOWPOS_CENTERED, 640,
      480, SDL_WINDOW_SHOWN))
      {
        g_bRunning = true;
      }
      else
      {
        return 1; // something's wrong
      }

      while(g_bRunning)
      {
        render();
      }

      // clean up SDL
      SDL_Quit();

      return 0;
    }
```

As you can see, we have broken the code up into separate parts: one function does the initialization for us and the other does the rendering code. We've added a way to keep the program running in the form of a `while` loop that runs continuously, rendering our window.

Getting Started with SDL

Let's take it a step further and try to identify which separate parts a full game might have and how our main loop might look. Referring to the first screenshot, we can see that the functions we will need are `initialize`, `get input`, `do physics`, `render`, and `exit`. We will generalize these functions slightly and rename them to `init()`, `handleEvents()`, `update()`, `render()`, and `clean()`. Let's put these functions into `main.cpp`:

```cpp
void init(){}
void render(){}
void update(){}
void handleEvents(){}
void clean(){}

bool g_bRunning = true;

int main()
{
   init();

   while(g_bRunning)
   {
      handleEvents();
      update();
      render();
   }

   clean();
}
```

What does this code do?

This code does not do much at the moment, but it shows the bare bones of a game and how a main loop might be broken apart. We declare some functions that can be used to run our game: first, the `init()` function, which will initialize SDL and create our window, and second, we declare the core loop functions of `render`, `update`, and `handle events`. We also declare a `clean` function, which will clean up code at the end of our game. We want this loop to continue running so we have a Boolean value that is set to `true`, so that we can continuously call our core loop functions.

The Game class

So, now that we have an idea of what makes up a game, we can separate the functions into their own class by following these steps:

1. Go ahead and create a new file in the project called `Game.h`:

    ```
    #ifndef __Game__
    #define __Game__

    class Game
    {
    };

    #endif /* defined(__Game__) */
    ```

2. Next, we can move our functions from the `main.cpp` file into the `Game.h` header file:

    ```
    class Game
    {
    public:

      Game() {}
      ~Game() {}

      // simply set the running variable to true
      void init() { m_bRunning = true; }

      void render(){}
      void update(){}
      void handleEvents(){}
      void clean(){}

      // a function to access the private running variable
      bool running() { return m_bRunning; }

    private:

      bool m_bRunning;
    };
    ```

Getting Started with SDL

3. Now, we can alter the `main.cpp` file to use this new `Game` class:

```cpp
#include "Game.h"

// our Game object
Game* g_game = 0;

int main(int argc, char* argv[])
{
  g_game = new Game();

  g_game->init("Chapter 1", 100, 100, 640, 480, 0);

  while(g_game->running())
  {
    g_game->handleEvents();
    g_game->update();
    g_game->render();
  }
  g_game->clean();

  return 0;
}
```

Our `main.cpp` file now does not declare or define any of these functions; it simply creates an instance of `Game` and calls the needed methods.

4. Now that we have this skeleton code, we can go ahead and tie SDL into it to create a window; we will also add a small event handler so that we can exit the application rather than having to force it to quit. We will slightly alter our `Game.h` file to allow us to add some SDL specifics and to also allow us to use an implementation file instead of defining functions in the header:

```cpp
#include "SDL.h"

class Game
{
public:

  Game();
  ~Game();

  void init();

  void render();
```

```
    void update();
    void handleEvents();
    void clean();

    bool running() { return m_bRunning; }

private:

    SDL_Window* m_pWindow;
    SDL_Renderer* m_pRenderer;

    bool m_bRunning;
};
```

Looking back at the first part of this chapter (where we created an SDL window), we know that we need a pointer to an SDL_Window object that is set when calling SDL_CreateWindow, and a pointer to an SDL_Renderer object that is created by passing our window into SDL_CreateRenderer. The init function can be extended to use the same parameters as in the initial sample as well. This function will now return a Boolean value so that we can check whether SDL is initialized correctly:

```
bool init(const char* title, int xpos, int ypos, int width, int height, int flags);
```

We can now create a new implementation Game.cpp file in the project so that we can create the definitions for these functions. We can take the code from the *Hello SDL* section and add it to the functions in our new Game class.

Open up Game.cpp and we can begin adding some functionality:

1. First, we must include our Game.h header file:

   ```
   #include "Game.h"
   ```

2. Next, we can define our init function; it is essentially the same as the init function we have previously written in our main.cpp file:

   ```
   bool Game::init(const char* title, int xpos, int ypos, int width, int height, int flags)
   {
     // attempt to initialize SDL
     if(SDL_Init(SDL_INIT_EVERYTHING) == 0)
     {
       std::cout << "SDL init success\n";
       // init the window
       m_pWindow = SDL_CreateWindow(title, xpos, ypos,
         width, height, flags);
   ```

```cpp
      if(m_pWindow != 0) // window init success
      {
        std::cout << "window creation success\n";
        m_pRenderer = SDL_CreateRenderer(m_pWindow, -1, 0);

        if(m_pRenderer != 0) // renderer init success
        {
          std::cout << "renderer creation success\n";
          SDL_SetRenderDrawColor(m_pRenderer,
            255,255,255,255);
        }
        else
        {
          std::cout << "renderer init fail\n";
          return false; // renderer init fail
        }
      }
      else
      {
        std::cout << "window init fail\n";
        return false; // window init fail
      }
    }
    else
    {
      std::cout << "SDL init fail\n";
      return false; // SDL init fail
    }

    std::cout << "init success\n";
    m_bRunning = true; // everything inited successfully,
    start the main loop

    return true;
  }
```

3. We will also define the `render` function. It clears the renderer and then renders again with the clear color:

```cpp
void Game::render()
{
  SDL_RenderClear(m_pRenderer); // clear the renderer to
  the draw color

  SDL_RenderPresent(m_pRenderer); // draw to the screen
}
```

4. Finally, we can clean up. We destroy both the window and the renderer and also call the SDL_Quit function to close all the subsystems:

```
{
  std::cout << "cleaning game\n";
  SDL_DestroyWindow(m_pWindow);
  SDL_DestroyRenderer(m_pRenderer);
  SDL_Quit();
}
```

So we have moved the Hello SDL 2.0 code from the main.cpp file into a class called Game. We have freed up the main.cpp file to handle only the Game class; it knows nothing about SDL or how the Game class is implemented. Let's add one more thing to the class to allow us to close the application the regular way:

```
void Game::handleEvents()
{
  SDL_Event event;
  if(SDL_PollEvent(&event))
  {
    switch (event.type)
    {
      case SDL_QUIT:
        m_bRunning = false;
      break;

      default:
      break;
    }
  }
}
```

We will cover event handling in more detail in a forthcoming chapter. What this function now does is check if there is an event to handle, and if so, check if it is an SDL_QUIT event (by clicking on the cross to close a window). If the event is SDL_QUIT, we set the Game class' m_bRunning member variable to false. The act of setting this variable to false makes the main loop stop and the application move onto cleaning up and then exiting:

```
void Game::clean()
{
  std::cout << "cleaning game\n";
  SDL_DestroyWindow(m_pWindow);
  SDL_DestroyRenderer(m_pRenderer);
  SDL_Quit();
}
```

Getting Started with SDL

The `clean()` function destroys the window and renderer and then calls the `SDL_Quit()` function, closing all the initialized SDL subsystems.

> To enable us to view our `std::cout` messages, we must first include `Windows.h` and then call `AllocConsole();` and `freopen("CON", "w", stdout);`. You can do this in the `main.cpp` file. Just remember to remove it when sharing your game.

Fullscreen SDL

`SDL_CreateWindow` takes an enumeration value of type `SDL_WindowFlags`. These values set how the window will behave. We created an `init` function in our `Game` class:

```
bool init(const char* title, int xpos, int ypos, int width, int
height, int flags);
```

The final parameter is an `SDL_WindowFlags` value, which is then passed into the `SDL_CreateWindow` function when initializing:

```
// init the window
m_pWindow = SDL_CreateWindow(title, xpos, ypos, width, height, flags);
```

Here is a table of the `SDL_WindowFlags` function:

Flag	Purpose
SDL_WINDOW_FULLSCREEN	Make the window fullscreen
SDL_WINDOW_OPENGL	Window can be used with as an OpenGL context
SDL_WINDOW_SHOWN	The window is visible
SDL_WINDOW_HIDDEN	Hide the window
SDL_WINDOW_BORDERLESS	No border on the window
SDL_WINDOW_RESIZABLE	Enable resizing of the window
SDL_WINDOW_MINIMIZED	Minimize the window
SDL_WINDOW_MAXIMIZED	Maximize the window
SDL_WINDOW_INPUT_GRABBED	Window has grabbed input focus
SDL_WINDOW_INPUT_FOCUS	Window has input focus
SDL_WINDOW_MOUSE_FOCUS	Window has mouse focus
SDL_WINDOW_FOREIGN	The window was not created using SDL

Let's pass in `SDL_WINDOW_FULLSCREEN` to the `init` function and test out some fullscreen SDL. Open up the `main.cpp` file and add this flag:

```
g_game->init("Chapter 1", 100, 100, 640, 580, SDL_WINDOW_FULLSCREEN))
```

Build the application again and you should see that the window is fullscreen. To exit the application, it will have to be forced to quit (*Alt + F4* on Windows); we will be able to use the keyboard to quit the application in forthcoming chapters, but for now, we won't need fullscreen. One problem we have here is that we have now added something SDL specific to the `main.cpp` file. While we will not use any other frameworks in this book, in future we may want to use another. We can remove this SDL-specific flag and replace it with a Boolean value for whether we want fullscreen or not.

Replace the `int flags` parameter in our `Game init` function with a `boolfullscreen` parameter:

- The code snippet for `Game.h`:

  ```
  bool init(const char* title, int xpos, int ypos, int width, int height, bool fullscreen);
  ```

- The code snippet for `Game.cpp`:

  ```
  bool Game::init(const char* title, int xpos, int ypos, int width, int height, bool fullscreen)
  {
    int flags = 0;

    if(fullscreen)
    {
      flags = SDL_WINDOW_FULLSCREEN;
    }
  }
  ```

We create an `int` flags variable to pass into the `SDL_CreateWindow` function; if we have set `fullscreen` to `true`, then this value will be set to the `SDL_WINDOW_FULLSCREEN` flag, otherwise it will remain as `0` to signify that no flags are being used. Let's test this now in our `main.cpp` file:

```
if(g_game->init("Chapter 1", 100, 100, 640, 480, true))
```

This will again set our window to fullscreen, but we aren't using the SDL-specific flag to do it. Set it to `false` again as we will not need fullscreen for a while. Feel free to try out a few of the other flags to see what effects they have.

Summary

A lot of ground has been covered in this chapter. We learned what SDL is and why it is a great tool for game development. We looked at the overall structure of a game and how it can be broken into individual parts, and we started to develop the skeleton of our framework by creating a `Game` class that can be used to initialize SDL and render things to the screen. We also had a small look at how SDL handles events by listening for a `quit` event to close our application. In the next chapter we will look at drawing in SDL and building the `SDL_image` extension.

2
Drawing in SDL

Graphics are very important to games and they can also be one of the main performance bottlenecks if not handled correctly. With SDL 2.0 we can really take advantage of the GPU when rendering, which gives us a real boost in terms of the speed of rendering.

In this chapter we will cover:

- The basics of drawing with SDL
- Source and destination rectangles
- Loading and displaying textures
- Using the `SDL_image` extension

Basic SDL drawing

In the previous chapter we created an SDL window but we have yet to render anything to the screen. SDL can use two structures to draw to the screen. One is the `SDL_Surface` structure, which contains a collection of pixels and is rendered using software rendering processes (not the GPU). The other is `SDL_Texture`; this can be used for hardware-accelerated rendering. We want our games to be as efficient as possible so we will focus on using `SDL_Texture`.

Getting some images

We need some images to load throughout this chapter. We do not want to spend any time creating art assets for our games at this point; we want to focus entirely on the programming side. In this book we will use assets from the `SpriteLib` collection available at `http://www.widgetworx.com/widgetworx/portfolio/spritelib.html`.

Drawing in SDL

I have altered some of these files to allow us to easily use them in the upcoming chapters. These images are available with the source code download for this book. The first one we will use is the `rider.bmp` image file:

Creating an SDL texture

First we will create a pointer to an `SDL_Texture` object as a member variable in our `Game.h` header file. We will also create some rectangles to be used when drawing the texture.

```
SDL_Window* m_pWindow;
SDL_Renderer* m_pRenderer;

SDL_Texture* m_pTexture; // the new SDL_Texture variable
SDL_Rect m_sourceRectangle; // the first rectangle
SDL_Rect m_destinationRectangle; // another rectangle
```

We can load this texture in our game's `init` function for now. Open up `Game.cpp` and follow the steps to load and draw an `SDL_Texture`:

1. First we will make an assets folder to hold our images, place this in the same folder as your source code (not the executable code). When you want to distribute the game you will copy this assets folder along with your executable. But for development purposes we will keep it in the same folder as the source code. Place the `rider.bmp` file into this assets folder.

2. In our game's `init` function we can load our image. We will use the `SDL_LoadBMP` function which returns an `SDL_Surface*`. From this `SDL_Surface*` we can create `SDL_Texture` structure using the `SDL_CreateTextureFromSurface` function. We then free the temporary surface, releasing any used memory.

   ```
   SDL_Surface* pTempSurface = SDL_LoadBMP("assets/rider.bmp");

   m_pTexture = SDL_CreateTextureFromSurface(m_pRenderer,
   pTempSurface);

   SDL_FreeSurface(pTempSurface);
   ```

3. We now have `SDL_Texture` ready to be drawn to the screen. We will first get the dimensions of the texture we have just loaded, and use them to set the width and height of `m_sourceRectangle` so that we can draw it correctly.

   ```
   SDL_QueryTexture(m_pTexture, NULL, NULL,
   &m_sourceRectangle.w, &m_sourceRectangle.h);
   ```

4. Querying the texture will allow us to set the width and height of our source rectangle to the exact dimensions needed. So now that we have the correct height and width of our texture stored in `m_sourceRectangle` we must also set the destination rectangle's height and width. This is done so that our renderer knows which part of the window to draw our image to, and also the width and height of the image we want to render. We will set both x and y coordinates to 0 (top left). Window coordinates can be represented with an x and y value, with x being the horizontal position and y the vertical. Therefore the coordinates for the top-left of a window in SDL would be (0,0) and the center point would be the width of the window divided by two for x, and the height of the window divided by two for y.

   ```
   m_destinationRectangle.x = m_sourceRectangle.x = 0;
   m_destinationRectangle.y = m_sourceRectangle.y = 0;
   m_destinationRectangle.w = m_sourceRectangle.w;
   m_destinationRectangle.h = m_sourceRectangle.h;
   ```

5. Now that we have a loaded texture and its dimensions, we can move on to rendering it to the screen. Move to our game's `render` function and we will add the code to draw our texture. Put this function between the calls to `SDL_RenderClear` and `SDL_RenderPresent`.

   ```
   SDL_RenderCopy(m_pRenderer, m_pTexture, &m_sourceRectangle,
   &m_destinationRectangle);
   ```

6. Build the project and you will see our loaded texture.

Drawing in SDL

Source and destination rectangles

Now that we have something drawn to the screen, it is a good idea to cover the purpose of source and destination rectangles, as they will be extremely important for topics such as tile map loading and drawing. They are also important for sprite sheet animation which we will be covering later in this chapter.

We can think of a source rectangle as defining the area we want to copy from a texture onto the window:

1. In the previous example, we used the entire image so we could simply define the source rectangle's dimensions with the same dimensions as those of the loaded texture.

2. The red box in the preceding screenshot is a visual representation of the source rectangle we used when drawing to the screen. We want to copy pixels from inside the source rectangle to a specific area of the renderer, the destination rectangle (the red box in the following screenshot).

3. As you would expect, these rectangles can be defined however you wish. For example, let's open up our `Game.cpp` file again and take a look at changing the size of the source rectangle. Place this code after the `SDL_QueryTexture` function.

[32]

```
m_sourceRectangle.w = 50;
m_sourceRectangle.h = 50;
```

Now build again and you should see that only a 50 x 50 square of the image has been copied across to the renderer.

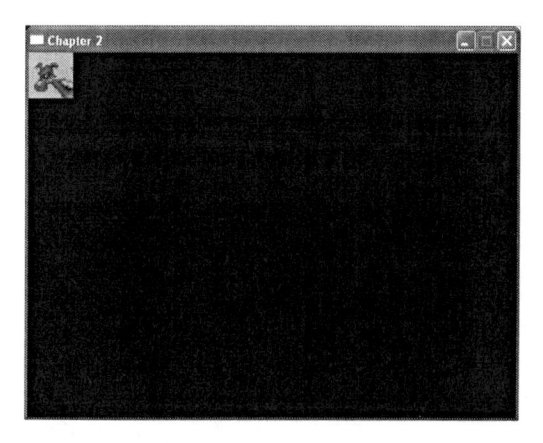

4. Now let us move the destination rectangle by changing its x and y values.

   ```
   m_destinationRectangle.x = 100;
   m_destinationRectangle.y = 100;
   ```

   Build the project again and you will see that our source rectangle location has remained the same but the destination rectangle has moved. All we have done is move the location that we want the pixels inside the source rectangle to be copied to.

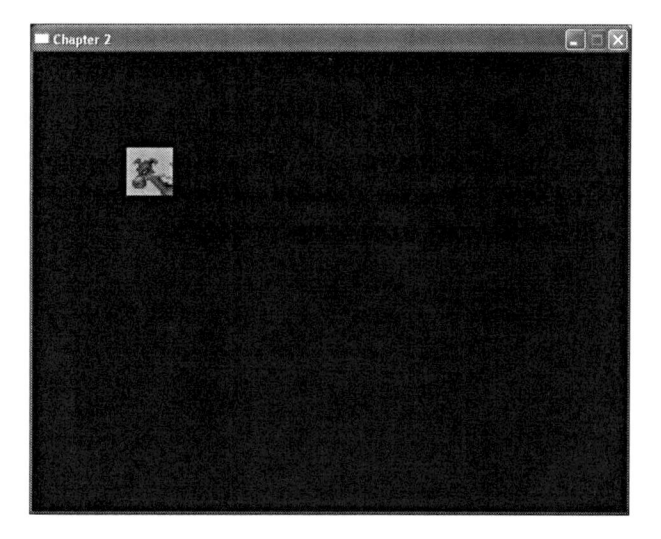

Drawing in SDL

5. So far we have left the source rectangle's x and y coordinates at 0 but they can also be moved around to only draw the section of the image that you want. We can move the x and y coordinates of the source to draw the bottom-right section of the image rather than the top-left. Place this code just before where we set the destination rectangle's location.

   ```
   m_sourceRectangle.x = 50;
   m_sourceRectangle.y = 50;
   ```

   You can see that we are still drawing to the same destination location but we are copying a different 50 x 50 section of the image.

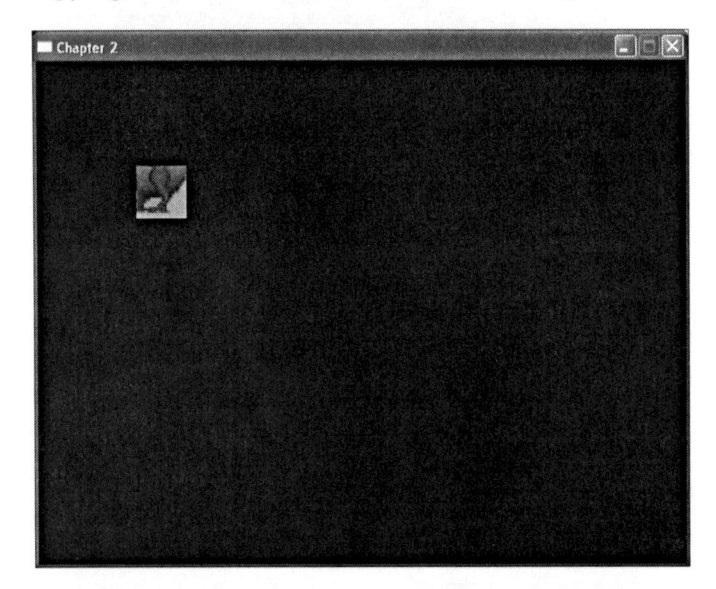

6. We can also pass null into the render copy for either rectangle.

   ```
   SDL_RenderCopy(m_pRenderer, m_pTexture, 0, 0);
   ```

   Passing null into the source rectangle parameter will make the renderer use the entire texture. Likewise, passing null to the destination rectangle parameter will use the entire renderer for display.

Chapter 2

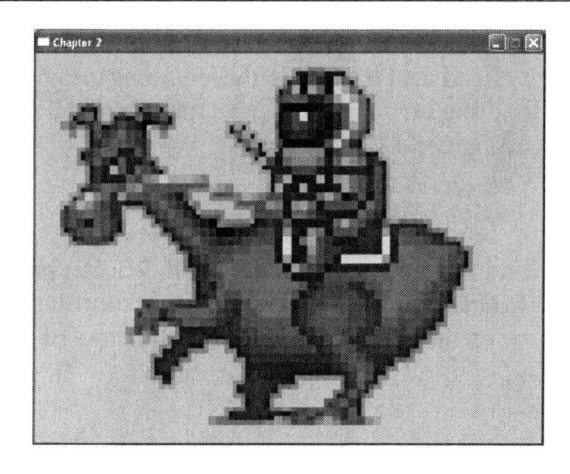

We have covered a few different ways that we can use rectangles to define areas of images that we would like to draw. We will now put that knowledge into practice by displaying an animated sprite sheet.

Animating a sprite sheet

We can apply our understanding of source and destination rectangles to the animation of a sprite sheet. A sprite sheet is a series of animation frames all put together into one image. The separate frames need to have a very specific width and height so that they create a seamless motion. If one part of the sprite sheet is not correct it will make the whole animation look out of place or completely wrong. Here is an example sprite sheet that we will use for this demonstration:

1. This animation is six frames long and each frame is 128 x 82 pixels. We know from the previous section that we can use a source rectangle to grab a certain part of an image. Therefore we can start by defining a source rectangle that encompasses the first frame of the animation only.

Drawing in SDL

2. Since we know the width, height, and location of the frame on the sprite sheet we can go ahead and hardcode these values into our source rectangle. First we must load the new `animate.bmp` file. Place it into your assets folder and alter the loading code.

   ```
   SDL_Surface* pTempSurface =
   SDL_LoadBMP("assets/animate.bmp");
   ```

3. This will now load our new sprite sheet BMP. We can remove the `SDL_QueryTexture` function as we are now defining our own sizes. Alter the size of the source rectangle to only get the first frame of the sheet.

   ```
   m_sourceRectangle.w = 128;
   m_sourceRectangle.h = 82;
   ```

4. We will leave the x and y position of both rectangles at 0 so that we draw the image from the top-left corner and also copy it to the top-left corner of the renderer. We will also leave the dimensions of the destination rectangle as we want it to remain the same as the source rectangle. Pass both rectangles into the `SDL_RenderCopy` function:

   ```
   SDL_RenderCopy(m_pRenderer, m_pTexture, &m_sourceRectangle,
   &m_destinationRectangle);
   ```

   Now when we build we will have the first frame of the animation.

Chapter 2

5. Now that we have the first frame, we can move on to animating the sprite sheet. Each frame has the exact same dimensions. This is extremely important for this sheet to animate correctly. All we want to do is move the location of the source rectangle, not its dimensions.

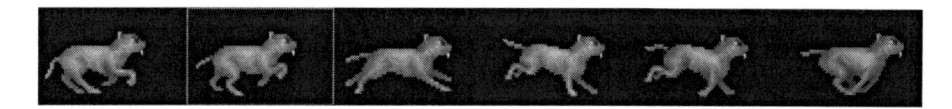

6. Every time we want to move another frame, we simply move the location of the source rectangle and copy it to the renderer. To do this we will use our `update` function.

   ```
   void Game::update()
   {
       m_sourceRectangle.x = 128 * int(((SDL_GetTicks() / 100) % 6));
   }
   ```

7. Here we have used `SDL_GetTicks()` to find out the amount of milliseconds since SDL was initialized. We then divide this by the amount of time (in ms) we want between frames and then use the modulo operator to keep it in range of the amount of frames we have in our animation. This code will (every 100 milliseconds) shift the x value of our source rectangle by 128 pixels (the width of a frame), multiplied by the current frame we want, giving us the correct position. Build the project and you should see the animation displayed.

Flipping images

In most games, players, enemies, and so on, will move in more than one direction. To allow the sprite to face in the direction it is moving we will have to flip our sprite sheet. We could of course create a new row in our sprite sheet with the frames flipped, but this would use more memory, which we do not want. SDL 2.0 has another render function that allows us to pass in the way we want our image to be flipped or rotated. The function we will use is `SDL_RenderCopyEx`. This function takes the same parameters as `SDL_RenderCopy` but also takes specific parameters for rotation and flipping. The fourth parameter is the angle we want the image to be displayed with parameter five being the center point we want for the rotation. The final parameter is an enumerated type called `SDL_RendererFlip`.

Drawing in SDL

The following table shows the available values for the `SDL_RendererFlip` enumerated type:

SDL_RendererFlip value	Purpose
`SDL_FLIP_NONE`	No flipping
`SDL_FLIP_HORIZONTAL`	Flip the texture horizontally
`SDL_FLIP_VERTICAL`	Flip the texture vertically

We can use this parameter to flip our image. Here is the revised render function:

```
void Game::render()
{
  SDL_RenderClear(m_pRenderer);

  SDL_RenderCopyEx(m_pRenderer, m_pTexture,
  &m_sourceRectangle, &m_destinationRectangle,
  0, 0, SDL_FLIP_HORIZONTAL); // pass in the horizontal flip

  SDL_RenderPresent(m_pRenderer);
}
```

Build the project and you will see that the image has been flipped and is now facing to the left. Our characters and enemies will also have frames specifically for animations such as attack and jump. These can be added to different rows of the sprite sheet and the source rectangle's y value is incremented accordingly. (We will cover this in more detail when we create our game objects.)

Installing SDL_image

So far we have only been loading BMP image files. This is all that SDL supports without any extensions. We can use `SDL_image` to enable us to load many different image file types such as BMP, GIF, JPEG, LBM, PCX, PNG, PNM, TGA, TIFF, WEBP, XCF, XPM, and XV. First we will need to clone the latest build of `SDL_image` to ensure it will work with SDL 2.0:

1. Open up the `TortoiseHg` workbench and use *Ctrl + Shift + N* to clone a new repository.
2. The repository for SDL_image is listed on `http://www.libsdl.org/projects/SDL_image/` and `http://hg.libsdl.org/SDL_image/`. So let's go ahead and type that into the **Source** box.

Chapter 2

3. Our destination will be a new directory, `C:\SDL2_image`. After typing this into the **Destination** box, hit **clone** and wait for it to complete.

4. Once you have created this folder, navigate to our `C:\SDL2_image` cloned repository. Open up the `VisualC` folder and then open the `SDL_image_VS2010` VC++ project with Visual Studio 2010 express.

5. Right-click on the `SDL2_image` project and then click on **Properties**. Here we have to include the `SDL.h` header file. Change the configuration to **All Configurations**, navigate to **VC++ Directories**, click on the **Include Directories** drop-down, and then on **<Edit...>**. Here we can put in our `C:\SDL2\include\` directory.

6. Next move to **Library Directories** and add our `C:\SDL2\lib\` folder. Now navigate to **Linker | Input | Additional Dependencies** and add `SDL2.lib`.

7. Click on **OK** and we are almost ready to build. We are now using `SDL2.lib`, so we can remove the `SDL.lib` and the `SDLmain.lib` files from the `SDL_image` project. Locate the files in the solution explorer, right-click and then remove the files. Change the build configuration to **release** and then build.

8. An error about being unable to start the program may appear. Just click on **OK** and we can close the project and continue.

9. There will now be a `Release` folder inside our `C:\SDL2_image\VisualC\` folder. Open it and copy the `SDL_image.dll` to our game's executable folder.

10. Next copy the `SDL2_image.lib` file into our original `C:\SDL2\lib\` directory. Also copy the `SDL_image` header from `C:\SDL2_image\` to the `C:\SDL2\include\` directory.

11. We just have a few more libraries to get and we are done. Download the `SDL_image-1.2.12-win32.zip` file (or the x64 if you are targeting a 64 bit platform) from http://www.libsdl.org/projects/SDL_image/. Extract all and then copy all of the `.dll` files apart from `SDL_image.dll` into our game's executable folder.

Drawing in SDL

12. Open up our game project and go into its properties. Navigate to **Linker | Input | Additional Dependencies** and add `SDL2_image.lib`.

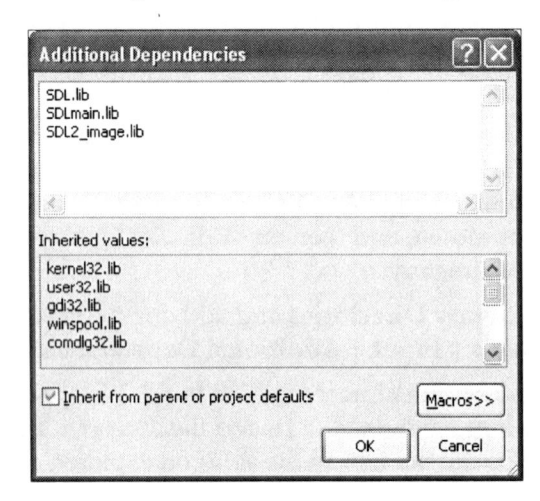

13. We have now installed `SDL_image` and can start to load all kinds of different image files. Copy the `animate.png` and `animate-alpha.png` images from the source downloads to our games assets folder and we can start loading PNG files.

Using SDL_image

So we have the library installed, now how do we use it? It is simple to use SDL_image in place of the regular SDL image loading. In our case we only need to replace one function and also add `#include <SDL_image.h>`.

```
SDL_Surface* pTempSurface = SDL_LoadBMP("assets/animate.bmp");
```

The preceding code will be changed as follows:

```
SDL_Surface* pTempSurface = IMG_Load("assets/animate.png");
```

We are now loading a `.png` image. PNG files are great to work with, they have a small file size and support an alpha channel. Let's perform a test. Change our renderer clear color to red.

```
SDL_SetRenderDrawColor(m_pRenderer, 255,0,0,255);
```

You will see that we still have our black background from the image we are using; this is definitely not ideal for our purposes.

When using PNG files, we can resolve this by using an alpha channel. We remove the background from the image and then when we load it, SDL will not draw anything from the alpha channel.

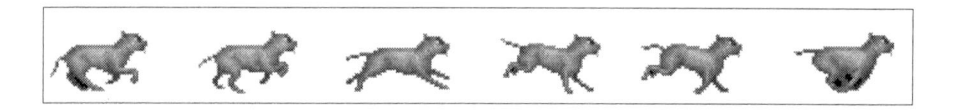

Let's load this image and see how it looks:

```
SDL_Surface* pTempSurface = IMG_Load("assets/animate-alpha.png");
```

This is exactly what we want:

Drawing in SDL

Tying it into the framework

We have covered a lot on the subject of drawing images with SDL but we have yet to tie everything together into our framework so that it becomes reusable throughout our game. What we will now cover is creating a texture manager class that will have all of the functions we need to easily load and draw textures.

Creating the texture manager

The texture manager will have functions that allow us to load and create an `SDL_Texture` structure from an image file, draw the texture (either static or animated), and also hold a list of `SDL_Texture*`, so that we can use them whenever we need to. Let's go ahead and create the `TextureManager.h` file:

1. First we declare our `load` function. As parameters, the function takes the filename of the image we want to use, the ID we want to use to refer to the texture, and the renderer we want to use.

   ```
   bool load(std::string fileName,std::string id,
   SDL_Renderer* pRenderer);
   ```

2. We will create two draw functions, `draw` and `drawFrame`. They will both take the ID of the texture we want to draw, the x and y position we want to draw to, the height and width of the frame or the image we are using, the renderer we will copy to, and an `SDL_RendererFlip` value to describe how we want the image to be displayed (default is `SDL_FLIP_NONE`). The `drawFrame` function will take two additional parameters, the current frame we want to draw and which row it is on in the sprite sheet.

   ```
   // draw
   void draw(std::string id, int x, int y, int width, int
   height, SDL_Renderer* pRenderer, SDL_RendererFlip flip =
   SDL_FLIP_NONE);

   // drawframe

   void drawFrame(std::string id, int x, int y, int width, int
   height, int currentRow, int currentFrame, SDL_Renderer*
   pRenderer, SDL_RendererFlip flip = SDL_FLIP_NONE);
   ```

3. The `TextureManager` class will also contain `std::map` of pointers to the `SDL_Texture` objects, keyed using `std::strings`.

   ```
   std::map<std::string, SDL_Texture*> m_textureMap;
   ```

4. We now must define these functions in a `TextureManager.cpp` file. Let's start with the `load` function. We will take the code from our previous texture loading and use it within this `load` method.

```
bool TextureManager::load(std::string fileName, std::string
id, SDL_Renderer* pRenderer)
{
  SDL_Surface* pTempSurface = IMG_Load(fileName.c_str());

  if(pTempSurface == 0)
  {
    return false;
  }

  SDL_Texture* pTexture =
  SDL_CreateTextureFromSurface(pRenderer, pTempSurface);

  SDL_FreeSurface(pTempSurface);

  // everything went ok, add the texture to our list
  if(pTexture != 0)
  {
    m_textureMap[id] = pTexture;
    return true;
  }

  // reaching here means something went wrong
  return false;
}
```

5. When we call this function we will then have `SDL_Texture` that can be used by accessing it from the map using its ID; we will use this in our `draw` functions. The `draw` function can be defined as follows:

```
void TextureManager::draw(std::string id, int x, int y, int
width, int height, SDL_Renderer* pRenderer,
SDL_RendererFlip flip)
{
  SDL_Rect srcRect;
  SDL_Rect destRect;

  srcRect.x = 0;
  srcRect.y = 0;
  srcRect.w = destRect.w = width;
```

[43]

Drawing in SDL

```
    srcRect.h = destRect.h = height;
    destRect.x = x;
    destRect.y = y;

    SDL_RenderCopyEx(pRenderer, m_textureMap[id], &srcRect,
    &destRect, 0, 0, flip);
}
```

6. We again use `SDL_RenderCopyEx` using the passed in ID variable to get the `SDL_Texture` object we want to draw. We also build our source and destination variables using the passed in x, y, width, and height values. Now we can move onto drawFrame:

```
void TextureManager::drawFrame(std::string id, int x, int y, int
width, int height, int currentRow, int currentFrame, SDL_Renderer
*pRenderer, SDL_RendererFlip flip)
{
    SDL_Rect srcRect;
    SDL_Rect destRect;
    srcRect.x = width * currentFrame;
    srcRect.y = height * (currentRow - 1);
    srcRect.w = destRect.w = width;
    srcRect.h = destRect.h = height;
    destRect.x = x;
    destRect.y = y;

    SDL_RenderCopyEx(pRenderer, m_textureMap[id], &srcRect,
    &destRect, 0, 0, flip);
}
```

In this function, we create a source rectangle to use the appropriate frame of the animation using the `currentFrame` and `currentRow` variables. The source rectangle's x position for the current frame is the width of the source rectangle multiplied by the `currentFrame` value (covered in the *Animating a sprite sheet* section). Its y value is the height of the rectangle multiplied by `currentRow - 1` (it sounds more natural to use the first row, rather than the zeroth row).

7. We now have everything we need to easily load and draw textures throughout our game. Let's go ahead and test it out using the `animated.png` image. Open up Game.h. We will not need our texture member variables or the rectangles anymore, so delete any of the code dealing with them from the Game.h and Game.cpp files. We will however create two new member variables.

```
int m_currentFrame;
TextureManager m_textureManager;
```

8. We will use the `m_currentFrame` variable to allow us to animate our sprite sheet and we also need an instance of our new `TextureManager` class (ensure you include `TextureManager.h`). We can now load a texture in the game's `init` function.

```
m_textureManager.load("assets/animate-alpha.png",
"animate", m_pRenderer);
```

9. We have given this texture an ID of `"animate"` which we can use in our `draw` functions. We will start by drawing a static image at 0,0 and an animated image at 100,100. Here is the render function:

```
void Game::render()
{
  SDL_RenderClear(m_pRenderer);

  m_textureManager.draw("animate", 0,0, 128, 82,
  m_pRenderer);

  m_textureManager.drawFrame("animate", 100,100, 128, 82,
  1, m_currentFrame, m_pRenderer);

  SDL_RenderPresent(m_pRenderer);

}
```

10. The drawFrame function uses our `m_currentFrame` member variable. We can increment this in the `update` function like we did before, but we now do the calculation of the source rectangle inside the `draw` function.

```
void Game::update()
{
  m_currentFrame = int(((SDL_GetTicks() / 100) % 6));
}
```

Now we can build and see our hard work in action.

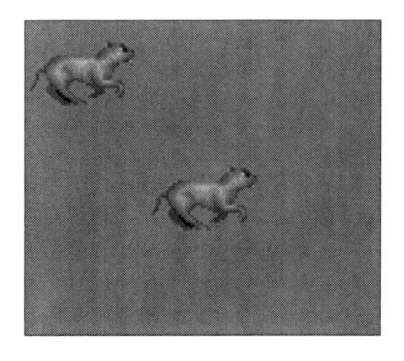

[45]

Drawing in SDL

Using texture manager as a singleton

Now that we have our texture manager in place we still have one problem. We want to reuse this `TextureManager` throughout our game so we don't want it to be a member of our `Game` class because then we would have to pass it into our draw function. A good option for us is to implement `TextureManager` as a singleton. A singleton is a class that can only have one instance. This works for us, as we want to reuse the same `TextureManager` throughout our game. We can make our `TextureManager` a singleton by first making its constructor private.

```
private:

TextureManager() {}
```

This is to ensure that it cannot be created like other objects. It can only be created and accessed using the `Instance` function, which we will declare and define.

```
static TextureManager* Instance()
{
  if(s_pInstance == 0)
  {
    s_pInstance = new TextureManager();
    return s_pInstance;
  }

  return s_pInstance;
}
```

This function checks whether we already have an instance of our `TextureManager`. If not, then it constructs it, otherwise it simply returns the static instance. We will also `typedef` the `TextureManager`.

```
typedef TextureManager TheTextureManager;
```

We must also define the static instance in `TextureManager.cpp`.

```
TextureManager* TextureManager::s_pInstance = 0;
```

We can now use our `TextureManager` as a singleton. We no longer have to have an instance of `TextureManager` in our `Game` class, we just include the header and use it as follows:

```
// to load
if(!TheTextureManager::Instance()->load("assets/animate-alpha.png",
"animate", m_pRenderer))
{
   return false;
}
// to draw
TheTextureManager::Instance()->draw("animate", 0,0, 128, 82,
m_pRenderer);
```

When we load a texture in our `Game` (or any other) class we can then access it throughout our code.

Summary

This chapter has been all about rendering images onto the screen. We have covered source and destination rectangles and animating a sprite sheet. We took what we learned and applied it to creating a reusable texture manager class, enabling us to easily load and draw images throughout our game. In the next chapter, we will cover using inheritance and polymorphism to create a base game object class and use it within our game framework.

3
Working with Game Objects

All games have objects, for example, players, enemies, **non-player character** (NPC), traps, bullets, and doors. Keeping track of all these objects and how they interact with each other is a big task and one that we would like to make as simple as possible. Our game could become unwieldy and difficult to update if we do not have a solid implementation. So what can we do to make our task easier? We can start by really trying to leverage the power of **object-oriented programming** (OOP). We will cover the following in this chapter:

- Using inheritance
- Implementing polymorphism
- Using abstract base classes
- Effective inheritance design

Using inheritance

The first powerful feature of OOP we will look at is inheritance. This feature can help us enormously when developing our reusable framework. Through the use of inheritance, we can share common functionality between similar classes and also create subtypes from existing types. We will not go into too much detail about inheritance itself but instead we will start to think about how we will apply it to our framework.

As mentioned earlier, all games have objects of various types. In most cases, these objects will have a lot of the same data and require a lot of the same basic functions. Let's look at some examples of this common functionality:

- Almost all of our objects will be drawn to the screen, thus requiring a `draw` function
- If our objects are to be drawn, they will need a location to draw to, that is, x and y position variables

Working with Game Objects

- We don't want static objects all the time, so we will need an `update` function
- Objects will be responsible for cleaning up after themselves; a function that deals with this will be important

This is a good starting point for our first game object class, so let's go ahead and create it. Add a new class to the project called `GameObject` and we can begin:

```
class GameObject
{
public:

  void draw() { std::cout << "draw game object"; }
  void update() { std::cout << "update game object"; }
  void clean() { std::cout << "clean game object"; }

protected:

  int m_x;
  int m_y;
};
```

> The public, protected, and private keywords are very important. Public functions and data are accessible from anywhere. Protected status restricts access to only those classes derived from it. Private members are only available to that class, not even its derived classes.

So, there we have our first game object class. Now let's inherit from it and create a class called `Player`:

```
class Player : public GameObject // inherit from GameObject
{
public:

  void draw()
  {
    GameObject::draw();
    std::cout << "draw player";
  }
  void update()
  {
    std::cout << "update player";
    m_x = 10;
    m_y = 20;
  }
  void clean()
```

[50]

```
    {
      GameObject::clean();
      std::cout << "clean player";
    }
};
```

What we have achieved is the ability to reuse the code and data that we originally had in GameObject and apply it to our new Player class. As you can see, a derived class can override the functionality of a parent class:

```
void update()
{
  std::cout << "update player";
  m_x = 10;
  m_y = 20;
}
```

Or it can even use the functionality of the parent class, while also having its own additional functionality on top:

```
void draw()
{
  GameObject::draw();
  std::cout << "draw player";
}
```

Here we call the draw function from GameObject and then define some player-specific functionality.

> The :: operator is called the scope resolution operator and it is used to identify the specific place that some data or function resides.

Okay, so far our classes do not do much, so let's add some of our SDL functionality. We will add some drawing code to the GameObject class and then reuse it within our Player class. First we will update our GameObject header file with some new values and functions to allow us to use our existing SDL code:

```
class GameObject
{
public:

  void load(int x, int y, int width, int height, std::string textureID);
  void draw(SDL_Renderer* pRenderer);
  void update();
```

Working with Game Objects

```cpp
    void clean();

protected:

  std::string m_textureID;

  int m_currentFrame;
  int m_currentRow;

  int m_x;
  int m_y;

  int m_width;
  int m_height;
};
```

We now have some new member variables that will be set in the new `load` function. We are also passing in the `SDL_Renderer` object we want to use in our `draw` function. Let's define these functions in an implementation file and create `GameObject.cpp`:

First define our new `load` function:

```cpp
void GameObject::load(int x, int y, int width, int height, std::string textureID)
{
  m_x = x;
  m_y = y;
  m_width = width;
  m_height = height;
  m_textureID = textureID;

  m_currentRow = 1;
  m_currentFrame = 1;
}
```

Here we are setting all of the values we declared in the header file. We will just use a start value of 1 for our `m_currentRow` and `m_currentFrame` values. Now we can create our `draw` function that will make use of these values:

```cpp
void GameObject::draw(SDL_Renderer* pRenderer)
{
  TextureManager::Instance()->drawFrame(m_textureID, m_x, m_y,
    m_width, m_height, m_currentRow, m_currentFrame, pRenderer);
}
```

We grab the texture we want from `TextureManager` using `m_textureID` and draw it according to our set values. Finally we can just put something in our `update` function that we can override in the `Player` class:

```
void GameObject::update()
{
  m_x += 1;
}
```

Our `GameObject` class is complete for now. We can now alter the `Player` header file to reflect our changes:

```
#include "GameObject.h"

class Player : public GameObject
{
public:

  void load(int x, int y, int width, int height, std::string
  textureID);
  void draw(SDL_Renderer* pRenderer);
  void update();
  void clean();
};
```

We can now move on to defining these functions in an implementation file. Create `Player.cpp` and we'll walk through the functions. First we will start with the `load` function:

```
void Player::load(int x, int y, int width, int height, string
textureID)
{
  GameObject::load(x, y, width, height, textureID);
}
```

Here we can use our `GameObject::load` function. And the same applies to our `draw` function:

```
void Player::draw(SDL_Renderer* pRenderer)
{
  GameObject::draw(pRenderer);
}
```

Working with Game Objects

And let's override the `update` function with something different; let's animate this one and move it in the opposite direction:

```
void Player::update()
{
  m_x -= 1;
}
```

We are all set; we can create these objects in the `Game` header file:

```
GameObject m_go;
Player m_player;
```

Then load them in the `init` function:

```
m_go.load(100, 100, 128, 82, "animate");
m_player.load(300, 300, 128, 82, "animate");
```

They will then need to be added to the `render` and `update` functions:

```
void Game::render()
{

  SDL_RenderClear(m_pRenderer); // clear to the draw colour

  m_go.draw(m_pRenderer);
  m_player.draw(m_pRenderer);

  SDL_RenderPresent(m_pRenderer); // draw to the screen

}

void Game::update()
{
  m_go.update();
  m_player.update();
}
```

We have one more thing to add to make this run correctly. We need to cap our frame rate slightly; if we do not, then our objects will move far too fast. We will go into more detail about this in a later chapter, but for now we can just put a delay in our main loop. So, back in `main.cpp`, we can add this line:

```
while(g_game->running())
{
  g_game->handleEvents();
  g_game->update();
```

```
    g_game->render();

    SDL_Delay(10); // add the delay
}
```

Now build and run to see our two separate objects:

Our Player class was extremely easy to write, as we had already written some of the code in our GameObject class, along with the needed variables. You may have noticed, however, that we were copying code into a lot of places in the Game class. It requires a lot of steps to create and add a new object to the game. This is not ideal, as it would be easy to miss a step and also it will get extremely hard to manage and maintain when a game goes beyond having two or three different objects.

What we really want is for our Game class not to need to care about different types; then we could loop through all of our game objects in one go, with separate loops for each of their functions.

Implementing polymorphism

This leads us to our next OOP feature, polymorphism. What polymorphism allows us to do is to refer to an object through a pointer to its parent or base class. This may not seem powerful at first, but what this will allow us to do is essentially have our Game class need only to store a list of pointers to one type and any derived types can also be added to this list.

Working with Game Objects

Let us take our `GameObject` and `Player` classes as examples, with an added derived class, `Enemy`. In our `Game` class we have an array of `GameObject*`:

```
std::vector<GameObject*> m_gameObjects;
```

We then declare four new objects, all of which are `GameObject*`:

```
GameObject* m_player;
GameObject* m_enemy1;
GameObject* m_enemy2;
GameObject* m_enemy3;
```

In our `Game::init` function we can then create instances of the objects using their individual types:

```
m_player = new Player();
m_enemy1 = new Enemy();
m_enemy2 = new Enemy();
m_enemy3 = new Enemy();
```

Now they can be pushed into the array of `GameObject*`:

```
m_gameObjects.push_back(m_player);
m_gameObjects.push_back(m_enemy1);
m_gameObjects.push_back(m_enemy2);
m_gameObjects.push_back(m_enemy3);
```

The `Game::draw` function can now look something like this:

```
void Game::draw()
{
  for(std::vector<GameObject*>::size_type i = 0; i !=
  m_gameObjects.size(); i++)
  {
    m_gameObjects[i]->draw(m_pRenderer);
  }
}
```

Notice that we are looping through all of our objects and calling the `draw` function. The loop does not care that some of our objects are actually `Player` or `Enemy`; it handles them in the same manner. We are accessing them through a pointer to their base class. So, to add a new type, it simply needs to be derived from `GameObject`, and the `Game` class can handle it.

- So let's implement this for real in our framework. First we need a base class; we will stick with `GameObject`. We will have to make some changes to the class so that we can use it as a base class:

```
class GameObject
{
public:

    virtual void load(int x, int y, int width, int height,
    std::string textureID);
    virtual void draw(SDL_Renderer* pRenderer);
    virtual void update();
    virtual void clean();

protected:

    std::string m_textureID;

    int m_currentFrame;
    int m_currentRow;

    int m_x;
    int m_y;

    int m_width;
    int m_height;
};
```

Notice that we have now prefixed our functions with the virtual keyword. The virtual keyword means that when calling this function through a pointer, it uses the definition from the type of the object itself, not the type of its pointer:

```
void Game::draw()
{
  for(std::vector<GameObject*>::size_type i = 0; i !=
  m_gameObjects.size(); i++)
  {
    m_gameObjects[i]->draw(m_pRenderer);
  }
}
```

In other words, this function would always call the `draw` function contained in `GameObject`, neither `Player` nor `Enemy`. We would never have the overridden behavior that we want. The virtual keyword would ensure that the `Player` and `Enemy` draw functions are called.

Working with Game Objects

Now we have a base class, so let's go ahead and try it out in our Game class. We will start by declaring the objects in the Game header file:

```
GameObject* m_go;
GameObject* m_player;
```

Now declare along with our GameObject* array:

```
std::vector<GameObject*> m_gameObjects;
```

Now create and load the objects in the init function, then push them into the array:

```
m_go = new GameObject();
m_player = new Player();

m_go->load(100, 100, 128, 82, "animate");
m_player->load(300, 300, 128, 82, "animate");

m_gameObjects.push_back(m_go);
m_gameObjects.push_back(m_player);
```

So far, so good; we can now create a loop that will draw our objects and another that will update them. Now let's look at the render and update functions:

```
void Game::render()
{

  SDL_RenderClear(m_pRenderer); // clear to the draw colour

  // loop through our objects and draw them
  for(std::vector<GameObject*>::size_type i = 0; i !=
  m_gameObjects.size(); i++)
  {
    m_gameObjects[i]->draw(m_pRenderer);
  }

  SDL_RenderPresent(m_pRenderer); // draw to the screen

}

void Game::update()
{
  // loop through and update our objects
```

[58]

Chapter 3

```
    for(std::vector<GameObject*>::size_type i = 0; i !=
    m_gameObjects.size(); i++)
    {
      m_gameObjects[i]->update();
    }
}
```

As you can see, this is a lot tidier and also much easier to manage. Let us derive one more class from `GameObject` just so that we nail this concept down. Create a new class called `Enemy`:

```
class Enemy : public GameObject
{
public:

    void load(int x, int y, int width, int height, std::string
    textureID);
    void draw(SDL_Renderer* pRenderer);
    void update();
    void clean();
};
```

We will define the functions of this class the same as `Player` with only the `update` function as an exception:

```
void Enemy::update()
{
  m_y += 1;
  m_x += 1;
  m_currentFrame = int(((SDL_GetTicks() / 100) % 6));
}
```

Now let's add it to the game. First, we declare it as follows:

```
GameObject* m_enemy;
```

Then create, load, and add to the array:

```
m_enemy = new Enemy();
m_enemy->load(0, 0, 128, 82, "animate");
m_gameObjects.push_back(m_enemy);
```

Working with Game Objects

We have just added a new type and it was extremely quick and simple. Run the game to see our three objects, each with their own different behavior.

We have covered a lot here and have a really nice system for handling our game objects, yet we still have an issue. There is nothing stopping us from deriving a class without the `update` or `draw` functions that we are using here, or even declaring a different function and putting the `update` code in there. It is unlikely that we, as the developers, would make this mistake, but others using the framework may. What we would like is the ability to force our derived classes to have their own implementation of a function we decide upon, creating something of a blueprint that we want all of our game objects to follow. We can achieve this through the use of an abstract base class.

Using abstract base classes

If we are to implement our design correctly, then we have to be certain that all of our derived classes have a declaration and definition for each of the functions we want to access through the base class pointer. We can ensure this by making `GameObject` an abstract base class. An abstract base class cannot be initialized itself; its purpose is to dictate the design of derived classes. This gives us reusability as we know that any object we derive from `GameObject` will immediately work in the overall scheme of the game.

An abstract base class is a class that contains at least one pure virtual function. A pure virtual function is a function that has no definition and must be implemented in any derived classes. We can make a function pure virtual by suffixing it with =0.

Should we always use inheritance?

Inheritance and polymorphism are both very useful and really show off the power of object-oriented programming. However, in some circumstances, inheritance can cause more problems than it solves, and therefore, we should bear in mind a few rules of thumb when deciding whether or not to use it.

Could the same thing be achieved with a simpler solution?

Let's say we want to make a more powerful `Enemy` object; it will have the same behavior a regular `Enemy` object will have but with more health. One possible solution would be to derive a new class `PowerEnemy` from `Enemy` and give it double health. In this solution the new class will seem extremely sparse; it will use the functionality from `Enemy` but with one different value. An easier solution would be to have a way to set the health of an `Enemy` class, whether through an accessor or in the constructor. Inheritance isn't needed at all.

Derived classes should model the "is a" relationship

When deriving a class, it is a good idea for it to model the "is a" relationship. This means that the derived class should also be of the same type as the parent class. For example, deriving a `Player2` class from `Player` would fit the model, as `Player2` "is a" `Player`. But let's say, for example, we have a `Jetpack` class and we derive `Player` from this class to give it access to all the functionality that a `Jetpack` class has. This would not model the "is a" relationship, as a `Player` class is not a `Jetpack` class. It makes a lot more sense to say a `Player` class has a `Jetpack` class, and therefore, a `Player` class should have a member variable of type `Jetpack` with no inheritance; this is known as containment.

Possible performance penalties

On platforms such as PC and Mac, the performance penalties of using inheritance and virtual functions are negligible. However, if you are developing for less powerful devices such as handheld consoles, phones, or embedded systems, this is something that you should take into account. If your core loop involves calling a virtual function many times per second, the performance penalties can add up.

Putting it all together

We can now put all of this knowledge together and implement as much as we can into our framework, with reusability in mind. We have quite a bit of work to do, so let's start with our abstract base class, GameObject. We are going to strip out anything SDL-specific so that we can reuse this class in other SDL projects if needed. Here is our stripped down GameObject abstract base class:

```
class GameObject
{
public:

   virtual void draw()=0;
   virtual void update()=0;
   virtual void clean()=0;

protected:

   GameObject(const LoaderParams* pParams) {}
   virtual ~GameObject() {}
};
```

The pure virtual functions have been created, forcing any derived classes to also declare and implement them. There is also now no load function; the reason for this is that we don't want to have to create a new load function for each new project. We can be pretty sure that we will need different values when loading our objects for different games. The approach we will take here is to create a new class called LoaderParams and pass that into the constructor of our objects.

LoaderParams is simply a class that takes values into its constructor and sets them as member variables that can then be accessed to set the initial values of an object. While it may just seem that we are moving the parameters from the load function to somewhere else, it is a lot easier to just create a new LoaderParams class than to track down and alter the load function of all of our objects.

So here is our `LoaderParams` class:

```
class LoaderParams
{
public:

  LoaderParams(int x, int y, int width, int height, std::string
  textureID) : m_x(x), m_y(y), m_width(width), m_height(height),
  m_textureID(textureID)
  {

  }

  int getX() const { return m_x; }
  int getY() const { return m_y; }
  int getWidth() const { return m_width; }
  int getHeight() const { return m_height; }
  std::string getTextureID() const { return m_textureID; }

private:

  int m_x;
  int m_y;

  int m_width;
  int m_height;

  std::string m_textureID;
};
```

This class holds any values we need when creating our object exactly the same way as our `load` function used to do.

We have also removed the `SDL_Renderer` parameter from the `draw` function. We will instead make our `Game` class a singleton, such as `TextureManager`. So, we can add the following to our `Game` class:

```
// create the public instance function
static Game* Instance()
{
  if(s_pInstance == 0)
  {
    s_pInstance = new Game();
    return s_pInstance;
  }
```

Working with Game Objects

```cpp
    return s_pInstance;
}
// make the constructor private
private:

  Game();
// create the s_pInstance member variable
  static Game* s_pInstance;

// create the typedef
  typedef Game TheGame;
```

In the `Game.cpp`, we have to define our static instance:

```cpp
Game* Game::s_pInstance = 0;
```

Let's also create a function in the header file that will return our `SDL_Renderer` object:

```cpp
SDL_Renderer* getRenderer() const { return m_pRenderer; }
```

Now that `Game` is a singleton, we are going to use it differently in our `main.cpp` file:

```cpp
int main(int argc, char* argv[])
{
  std::cout << "game init attempt...\n";
  if(TheGame::Instance()->init("Chapter 1", 100, 100, 640, 480,
  false))
  {
    std::cout << "game init success!\n";
    while(TheGame::Instance()->running())
    {
      TheGame::Instance()->handleEvents();
      TheGame::Instance()->update();
      TheGame::Instance()->render();

      SDL_Delay(10);
    }
  }
  else
  {
    std::cout << "game init failure - " << SDL_GetError() << "\n";
    return -1;
  }
```

```
        std::cout << "game closing...\n";
        TheGame::Instance()->clean();

        return 0;
}
```

Now when we want to access the m_pRenderer value from Game, we can use the getRenderer function. Now that GameObject is essentially empty, how do we achieve the code-sharing we originally had? We are going to derive a new generic class from GameObject and call it SDLGameObject:

```
class SDLGameObject : public GameObject
{
public:

    SDLGameObject(const LoaderParams* pParams);

    virtual void draw();
    virtual void update();
    virtual void clean();

protected:

    int m_x;
    int m_y;

    int m_width;
    int m_height;

    int m_currentRow;
    int m_currentFrame;

    std::string m_textureID;
};
```

With this class we can create our reusable SDL code. First, we can use our new LoaderParams class to set our member variables:

```
SDLGameObject::SDLGameObject(const LoaderParams* pParams) :
GameObject(pParams)
{
    m_x = pParams->getX();
    m_y = pParams->getY();
    m_width = pParams->getWidth();
    m_height = pParams->getHeight();
```

Working with Game Objects

```
    m_textureID = pParams->getTextureID();

    m_currentRow = 1;
    m_currentFrame = 1;
}
```

We can also use the same `draw` function as before, making use of our singleton `Game` class to get the renderer we want:

```
void SDLGameObject::draw()
{
    TextureManager::Instance()->drawFrame(m_textureID, m_x, m_y,
    m_width, m_height, m_currentRow, m_currentFrame,
    TheGame::Instance()->getRenderer());
}
```

`Player` and `Enemy` can now inherit from `SDLGameObject`:

```
class Player : public SDLGameObject
{
public:

    Player(const LoaderParams* pParams);

    virtual void draw();
    virtual void update();
    virtual void clean();
};
// Enemy class
class Enemy : public SDLGameObject
{
public:

    Enemy(const LoaderParams* pParams);

    virtual void draw();
    virtual void update();
    virtual void clean();
};
```

The `Player` class can be defined like so (the `Enemy` class is very similar):

```
Player::Player(const LoaderParams* pParams) :
SDLGameObject(pParams)
{
```

```
}

void Player::draw()
{
  SDLGameObject::draw(); // we now use SDLGameObject
}

void Player::update()
{
  m_x -= 1;
  m_currentFrame = int(((SDL_GetTicks() / 100) % 6));
}

void Player::clean()
{
}
```

Now that everything is in place, we can go ahead and create the objects in our Game class and see everything in action. We won't add the objects to the header file this time; we will use a shortcut and build our objects in one line in the init function:

```
m_gameObjects.push_back(new Player(new LoaderParams(100, 100, 128, 82, "animate")));

m_gameObjects.push_back(new Enemy(new LoaderParams(300, 300, 128, 82, "animate")));
```

Build the project. We now have everything in place to allow us to easily reuse our Game and GameObject classes.

Summary

We have covered a lot of complex subjects in this chapter, and the concepts and ideas will take some time to sink in. We have covered the ability to easily create classes without having to rewrite a lot of similar functionality and the use of inheritance and how it allows us to share code between similar classes. We looked at polymorphism and how it can make object management a lot cleaner and reusable while abstract base classes took our inheritance knowledge up a notch by creating the blueprint we want all of our objects to follow. Finally, we put all our new knowledge into the context of our framework.

4
Exploring Movement and Input Handling

We have already covered drawing to the screen and how to handle objects but we have not had anything moving around very much yet. Getting input from the user and then controlling our game objects is one of the most important topics in game development. It can decide the feel and responsiveness of your game and is something that a user can really pick up on. In this chapter we will cover:

- Cartesian coordinate systems
- 2D vectors
- Creating variables to control the movement of a game object
- Setting up a simple movement system
- Setting up input handling from joysticks, keyboard, and mouse
- Creating a fixed frame rate

Exploring Movement and Input Handling

Setting up game objects for movement

In the previous chapter, we gave our objects x and y values which we could then use to pass into our drawing code. The x and y values we used can be represented using a Cartesian coordinate system.

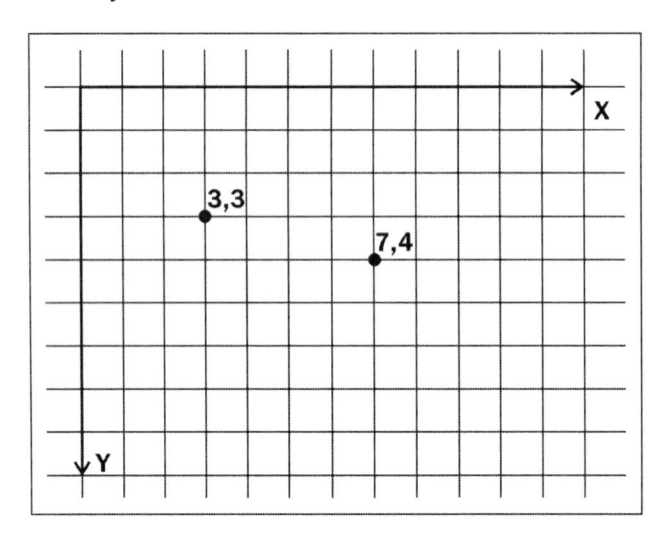

The above figure shows a Cartesian coordinate system (flipped on the Y axis) with two coordinates. Representing them as (x,y) gives us position 1 as (3,3) and position 2 as (7,4). These values can be used to represent a position in 2D space. Imagine this figure as a zoomed in image of the top-left corner of our game window, with each of the grid squares representing one pixel of our game window. With this in mind, we can see how to use these values to draw things to the screen in the correct position. We now need a way to update these position values so that we can move our objects around. For this we will look at 2D vectors.

What is a vector?

A **vector** can be described as an entity with a direction and a magnitude. We can use them to represent aspects of our game objects, for example, velocity and acceleration, that can be used to create movement. Taking velocity as an example, to fully represent the velocity of our objects, we need the direction in which they are travelling and also the amount (or magnitude) by which they are heading in that direction.

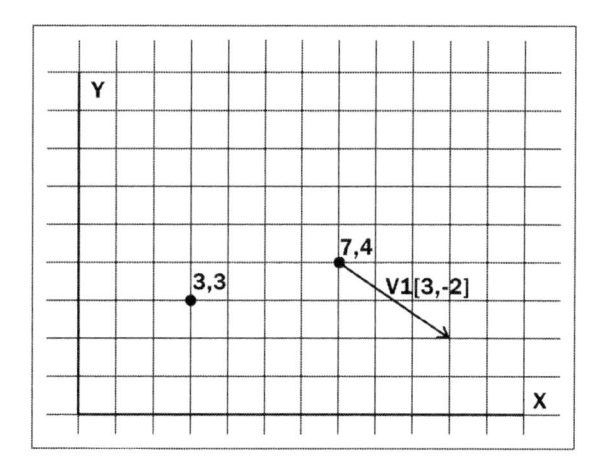

Let's define a couple of things about how we will use vectors:

- We will represent a vector as v(x,y)

  We can get the length of a vector using the following equation:

$$lengthofv(x,y) = \sqrt{(x^2 + y^2)}$$

The preceding figure shows the vector v1(3,-2) which will have a length of √(32+ (-22)). We can use the x and y components of a vector to represent our object's position in 2D space. We can then use some common vector operations to move our objects. Before we move onto these operations let's create a vector class called `Vector2D` in the project. We can then look at each operation we will need and add them to the class.

```
#include<math.h>
class Vector2D
{
public:
  Vector2D(float x, float y): m_x(x), m_y(y) {}

  float getX() { return m_x; }
  float getY() { return m_y; }

  void setX(float x) { m_x = x; }
  void setY(float y) { m_y = y; }
private:

  float m_x;
  float m_y;
};
```

Exploring Movement and Input Handling

You can see that the `Vector2D` class is very simple at this point. We have our x and y values and a way to get and set them. We already know how to get the length of a vector, so let's create a function for this purpose:

```
float length() { return sqrt(m_x * m_x + m_y * m_y); }
```

Some common operations

Now since we have our basic class in place, we can start to gradually add some operations.

Addition of two vectors

The first operation we will look at is the addition of two vectors. For this we simply add together the individual components of each vector.

$$v_3 = v_1 + v_2 = (x_1, y_1) + (x_2, y_2) = (x_1 + x_2, y_1 + y_2)$$

Let's make use of overloaded operators to make it easy for us to add two vectors together:

```
Vector2D operator+(const Vector2D& v2) const
{
   return Vector2D(m_x + v2.m_x, m_y + v2.m_y);
}

friend Vector2D& operator+=(Vector2D& v1, const Vector2D& v2)
{
   v1.m_x += v2.m_x;
   v1.m_y += v2.m_y;

   return v1;
}
```

With these functions we can add two vectors together using the standard addition operators, for example:

```
Vector2D v1(10, 11);
Vector2D v2(35,25);
v1 += v2;
Vector2D v3 = v1 + v2;
```

Multiply by a scalar number

Another operation is to multiply a vector by a regular scalar number. For this operation we multiply each component of the vector by the scalar number:

$$v_1 * n = (x_1 * n, y_1 * n)$$

We can again use overloaded operators to create these functions:

```
Vector2D operator*(float scalar)
{
   return Vector2D(m_x * scalar, m_y * scalar);
}

Vector2D& operator*=(float scalar)
{
   m_x *= scalar;
   m_y *= scalar;

   return *this;
}
```

Subtraction of two vectors

Subtraction is very similar to addition.

$$v_3 = v_1 - v_2 = (x_1, y_1) - (x_2, y_2) = (x_1 - x_2, y_1 - y_2)$$

Let's create some functions to do this for us:

```
Vector2D operator-(const Vector2D& v2) const
{
   return Vector2D(m_x - v2.m_x, m_y - v2.m_y);
}

friend Vector2D& operator-=(Vector2D& v1, const Vector2D& v2)
{
   v1.m_x -= v2.m_x;
   v1.m_y -= v2.m_y;

   return v1;
}
```

Divide by a scalar number

By now I am sure you have noticed a pattern emerging and can guess how dividing a vector by a scalar will work, but we will cover it anyway.

$$\frac{v_1}{n} = \left(\frac{x_1}{n}, \frac{y_1}{n}\right)$$

And our functions:

```
Vector2D operator/(float scalar)
{
  return Vector2D(m_x / scalar, m_y / scalar);
}

Vector2D& operator/=(float scalar)
{
  m_x /= scalar;
  m_y /= scalar;

  return *this;
}
```

Normalizing a vector

We need another very important operation and that is the ability to normalize a vector. Normalizing a vector makes its length equal to 1. Vectors with a length (magnitude) of 1 are known as unit vectors and are useful to represent just a direction, such as the facing direction of an object. To normalize a vector we multiply it by the inverse of its length.

$$l = length. \quad v_{normalized} = v_1 * 1/l$$

We can create a new member function to normalize our vectors:

```
void normalize()
{
  float l = length();
  if ( l > 0) // we never want to attempt to divide by 0
  {
    (*this) *= 1 / l;
  }
}
```

Now that we have a few basic functions in place, let's start to use these vectors in our `SDLGameObject` class.

Adding the Vector2D class

1. Open up `SDLGameObject.h` and we can begin implementing the vectors. First we need to include the new `Vector2D` class.

   ```
   #include "Vector2D.h"
   ```

2. We also need to remove the previous `m_x` and `m_y` values and replace them with `Vector2D`.

   ```
   Vector2D m_position;
   ```

3. Now we can move to the `SDLGameObject.cpp` file and update the constructor.

   ```
   SDLGameObject::SDLGameObject(const LoaderParams* pParams) :
   GameObject(pParams), m_position(pParams->getX(), pParams->getY())
   {
     m_width = pParams->getWidth();
     m_height = pParams->getHeight();
     m_textureID = pParams->getTextureID();

     m_currentRow = 1;
     m_currentFrame = 1;
   }
   ```

4. We now construct the `m_position` vector using the member initialization list and we must also use the `m_position` vector in our draw function.

   ```
   void SDLGameObject::draw()
   {
     TextureManager::Instance()->drawFrame(m_textureID,
     (int)m_position.getX(), (int)m_position.getY(), m_width,
     m_height, m_currentRow, m_currentFrame,
     TheGame::Instance()->getRenderer());
   }
   ```

5. One last thing before we test is to use our vector in the `Enemy::update` function.

   ```
   void Enemy::update()
   {
     m_position.setX(m_position.getX() + 1);
     m_position.setY(m_position.getY() + 1);
   }
   ```

Exploring Movement and Input Handling

This function will use vector addition very soon, but for now we just add 1 to the current position to get the same behavior we already had. We can now run the game and we will see that we have implemented a very basic vector system. Go ahead and play around with the `Vector2D` functions.

Adding velocity

We previously had to separately set the x and y values of our objects, but now that our position is a vector, we have the ability to add a new vector to it to update our movement. We will call this vector the velocity vector and we can think of it as the amount we want our object to move in a specific direction:

1. The velocity vector can be represented as follows:

$$v_{position} + v_{velocity} = (x_{position} + x_{velocity}, y_{position} + y_{velocity})$$

2. We can add this to our `SDLGameObject` update function as this is the way we update all derived objects. So first let's create the velocity member variable.

   ```
   Vector2D m_velocity;
   ```

3. We will construct it in the member initialization list as 0,0.

   ```
   SDLGameObject::SDLGameObject(const LoaderParams* pParams) :
   GameObject(pParams), m_position(pParams->getX(), pParams->getY()), m_velocity(0,0)
   ```

4. And now we will move to the `SDLGameObject::update` function.

   ```
   void SDLGameObject::update()
   {
     m_position += m_velocity;
   }
   ```

5. We can test this out in one of our derived classes. Move to `Player.cpp` and add the following:

   ```
   void Player::update()
   {
     m_currentFrame = int(((SDL_GetTicks() / 100) % 6));

     m_velocity.setX(1);

     SDLGameObject::update();
   }
   ```

We set the `m_velocity` x value to 1. This means that we will add 1 to our `m_position` x value each time the update function is called. Now we can run this to see our object move using the new velocity vector.

Adding acceleration

Not all of our objects will move along at a constant velocity. Some games will require that we gradually increase the velocity of our object using acceleration. A car or a spaceship are good examples. No one would expect these objects to hit their top speed instantaneously. We are going to need a new vector for acceleration, so let's add this into our `SDLGameObject.h` file.

```
Vector2D m_acceleration;
```

Then we can add it to our `update` function.

```
void SDLGameObject::update()
{
  m_velocity += m_acceleration;
  m_position += m_velocity;
}
```

Now alter our `Player::update` function to set the acceleration rather than the velocity.

```
void Player::update()
{
  m_currentFrame = int(((SDL_GetTicks() / 100) % 6));

  m_acceleration.setX(1);

  SDLGameObject::update();
}
```

After running our game you will see that the object gradually picks up speed.

Creating fixed frames per second

Earlier in the book we put in an `SDL_Delay` function to slow everything down and ensure that our objects weren't moving too fast. We will now expand upon that by making our game run at a fixed frame rate. Fixed frames per second (FPS) is not necessarily always a good option, especially when your game includes more advanced physics. It is worth bearing this in mind when you move on from this book and start developing your own games. Fixed FPS will, however, be fine for the small 2D games, which we will work towards in this book.

Exploring Movement and Input Handling

With that said, let's move on to the code:

1. Open up `main.cpp` and we will create a few constant variables.
   ```
   const int FPS = 60;
   const int DELAY_TIME = 1000.0f / FPS;

   int main()
   {
   ```

2. Here we define how many frames per second we want our game to run at. A frame rate of 60 frames per second is a good starting point as this is essentially synced up to the refresh rate of most modern monitors and TVs. We can then divide this by the number of milliseconds in a second, giving us the amount of time we need to delay the game between loops to keep our constant frame rate. We need another two variables at the top of our main function; these will be used in our calculations.
   ```
   int main()
   {
       Uint32 frameStart, frameTime;
   ```

3. We can now implement our fixed frame rate in our main loop.
   ```
   while(TheGame::Instance()->running())
   {
     frameStart = SDL_GetTicks();

     TheGame::Instance()->handleEvents();
     TheGame::Instance()->update();
     TheGame::Instance()->render();

     frameTime = SDL_GetTicks() - frameStart;

     if(frameTime< DELAY_TIME)
     {
       SDL_Delay((int)(DELAY_TIME - frameTime));
     }
   }
   ```

First we get the time at the start of our loop and store it in `frameStart`. For this we use `SDL_GetTicks` which returns the amount of milliseconds since we called `SDL_Init`. We then run our game loop and store how long it took to run by subtracting the time our frame started from the current time. If it is less than the time we want a frame to take, we call `SDL_Delay` and make our loop wait for the amount of time we want it to, subtracting how long the loop already took to complete.

Input handling

We have now got our objects moving based on velocity and acceleration, so next we must introduce some way of controlling this movement through user input. SDL supports a number of different types of user interface devices including joysticks, gamepads, mouse, and keyboard, all of which will be covered in this chapter, along with how to add them into our framework implementation.

Creating our input handler class

We will create a class that handles all device input, whether it is from controllers, keyboard, or mouse. Let's start with a basic class and build from there. First we need a header file, `InputHandler.h`.

```cpp
#include "SDL.h"
class InputHandler
{
public:
  static InputHandler* Instance()
  {
    if(s_pInstance == 0)
    {
      s_pInstance = new InputHandler();
    }

    return s_pInstance;
  }

  void update();
  void clean();

private:

  InputHandler();
  ~InputHandler() {}

  static InputHandler* s_pInstance;
};
typedef InputHandler TheInputHandler;
```

This is our singleton `InputHandler`. So far we have an `update` function which will poll for events and update our `InputHandler` accordingly, and a clean function which will clear any devices we have initialized. As we start adding device support we will flesh this out a lot more.

Handling joystick/gamepad input

There are tons of joysticks and gamepads out there, often with different amounts of buttons and analog sticks amongst other things. PC game developers have a lot to do when trying to support all of these different gamepads. SDL has good support for joysticks and gamepads, so we should be able to come up with a system that would not be difficult to extend for different gamepad support.

SDL joystick events

There are a few different structures for handling joystick events in SDL. The table below lists each one and their purpose.

SDL joystick event	Purpose
SDL_JoyAxisEvent	Axis motion information
SDL_JoyButtonEvent	Button press and release information
SDL_JoyBallEvent	Trackball event motion information
SDL_JoyHatEvent	Joystick hat position change

The events we are most interested in are the axis motion and the button press events. Each of these events also has an enumerated type that we can check for in our event loop to ensure we are only handling the events we want to handle. The table below shows the type value for each of the above events.

SDL joystick event	Type value
SDL_JoyAxisEvent	SDL_JOYAXISMOTION
SDL_JoyButtonEvent	SDL_JOYBUTTONDOWN or SDL_JOYBUTTONUP
SDL_JoyBallEvent	SDL_JOYBALLMOTION
SDL_JoyHatEvent	SDL_JOYHATMOTION

> It's a good idea to use the **Joystick Control Panel** property in Windows or **JoystickShow** on OSX to find out which button numbers you will need to use in SDL for a specific button. These applications are invaluable for finding out things about your joystick/gamepad so you can support them properly.

The code we will put in place will assume we are using a Microsoft Xbox 360 controller (which can be used on PC or OSX), as this is an extremely popular controller for PC gaming. Other controllers, such as the PS3 controller, could possibly have different values for buttons and axes. The Xbox 360 controller consists of the following:

- Two analog sticks
- Analog sticks press as buttons
- Start and Select buttons
- Four face buttons: A, B, X, and Y
- Four triggers: two digital and two analog
- A digital directional pad

Initializing joysticks

1. To use gamepads and joysticks in SDL we first need to initialize them. We are going to add a new public function to the InputHandler class. This function will find out how many joysticks SDL has access to and then initialize them.

    ```
    void initialiseJoysticks();
    bool joysticksInitialised() {
    return m_bJoysticksInitialised; }
    ```

2. We will also declare some private member variables that we will need.

    ```
    std::vector<SDL_Joystick*> m_joysticks;
    bool m_bJoysticksInitialised;
    ```

3. The SDL_Joystick* is a pointer to the joystick we will be initializing. We won't actually need these pointers when using the joysticks, but we do need to close them after we are done, so it is helpful for us to keep a list of them for later access. We will now define our initialiseJoysticks function and then go through it.

    ```
    void InputHandler::initialiseJoysticks()
    {
      if(SDL_WasInit(SDL_INIT_JOYSTICK) == 0)
      {
        SDL_InitSubSystem(SDL_INIT_JOYSTICK);
      }

      if(SDL_NumJoysticks() > 0)
      {
        for(int i = 0; i < SDL_NumJoysticks(); i++)
        {
          SDL_Joystick* joy = SDL_JoystickOpen(i);
    ```

Exploring Movement and Input Handling

```
        if(SDL_JoystickOpened(i) == 1)
        {
          m_joysticks.push_back(joy);
        }
        else
        {
          std::cout << SDL_GetError();
        }
      }
      SDL_JoystickEventState(SDL_ENABLE);
      m_bJoysticksInitialised = true;

      std::cout << "Initialised "<< m_joysticks.size() << "
      joystick(s)";
    }
    else
    {
      m_bJoysticksInitialised = false;
    }
  }
```

4. Let's go through this line-by-line. First we check whether the joystick subsystem has been initialized using `SDL_WasInit`. If it has not been initialized we then initialize it using `SDL_InitSubSystem`.

    ```
    if(SDL_WasInit(SDL_INIT_JOYSTICK) == 0)
    {
      SDL_InitSubSystem(SDL_INIT_JOYSTICK);
    }
    ```

5. Next is the opening of each available joystick. Before we attempt to open the objects, we use `SDL_NumJoysticks` to make sure there are some joysticks available. We can then loop through the number of joysticks, opening them in turn with `SDL_JoystickOpen`. They can then be pushed into our array for closing later.

    ```
    if(SDL_NumJoysticks() > 0)
    {
      for(int i = 0; i < SDL_NumJoysticks(); i++)
      {
        SDL_Joystick* joy = SDL_JoystickOpen(i);
        if(SDL_JoystickOpened(i))
        {
    ```

```
            m_joysticks.push_back(joy);
          }
          else
          {
            std::cout << SDL_GetError();
          }
        }
      }
    }
```

6. Finally, we tell SDL to start listening for joystick events by enabling SDL_ JoystickEventState. We also set our m_bJoysticksEnabled member variable according to how our initialization went.

```
    SDL_JoystickEventState(SDL_ENABLE);
    m_bJoysticksInitialised = true;

    std::cout << "Initialised " << m_joysticks.size() << " joystick(s)";

    }
    else
    {
      m_bJoysticksInitialised = false;
    }
```

7. So, we now have a way to initialize our joysticks. We have two other functions to define, the update and clean functions. The clean function will loop through our SDL_Joystick* array and call SDL_JoystickClose on each iteration.

```
    void InputHandler::clean()
    {
      if(m_bJoysticksInitialised)
      {
        for(unsigned int i = 0; i < SDL_NumJoysticks(); i++)
        {
          SDL_JoystickClose(m_joysticks[i]);
        }
      }
    }
```

8. The update function will be called in each frame in the main game loop to update the event state. For now though it will simply listen for a quit event and call the game's quit function (this function simply calls SDL_Quit()).

```
    void InputHandler::update()
    {
      SDL_Event event;
```

[83]

Exploring Movement and Input Handling

```
      while(SDL_PollEvent(&event))
      {
        if(event.type == SDL_QUIT)
        {
          TheGame::Instance()->quit();
        }
      }
    }
```

9. Now we will use this `InputHandler` in our `Game` class functions. First we call `initialiseJoysticks` in the `Game::init` function.

    `TheInputHandler::Instance()->initialiseJoysticks();`

    And we will update it in the `Game::handleEvents` function, clearing out anything we had before:

    ```
    void Game::handleEvents()
    {
      TheInputHandler::Instance()->update();
    }
    ```

10. The `clean` function can also be added to our `Game::clean` function.

    `TheInputHandler::Instance()->clean();`

11. We can now plug in a pad or joystick and run the build. If everything is working according to plan we should get the following output, with x being the number of joysticks you have plugged in:

    `Initialised x joystick(s)`

12. Ideally we want to easily use one or more controllers with no change to our code. We already have a way to load in and open as many controllers that are plugged in, but we need to know which event corresponds to which controller; we do this using some information stored in the event. Each joystick event will have a `which` variable stored within it. Using this will allow us to find out which joystick the event came from.

    ```
    if(event.type == SDL_JOYAXISMOTION) // check the type value
    {
      int whichOne = event.jaxis.which; // get which controller
    ```

Listening for and handling axis movement

We are not going to handle the analog sticks in an analog way. Instead they will be handled as digital information, that is, they are either on or off. Our controller has four axes of motion, two for the left analog stick and two for the right.

Chapter 4

We will make the following assumptions about our controller (you can use an external application to find out the specific values for your controller):

- Left and right movement on stick one is axis 0
- Up and down movement on stick one is axis 1
- Left and right movement on stick two is axis 3
- Up and down movement on stick two is axis 4

The Xbox 360 controller uses axes 2 and 5 for the analog triggers. To handle multiple controllers with multiple axes we will create a vector of pairs of Vector2D*, one for each stick.

```
std::vector<std::pair<Vector2D*, Vector2D*>> m_joystickValues;
```

We use the Vector2D values to set whether a stick has moved up, down, left, or right. Now when we initialize our joysticks we need to create a pair of Vector2D* in the m_joystickValues array.

```
for(int i = 0; i < SDL_NumJoysticks(); i++)
{
  SDL_Joystick* joy = SDL_JoystickOpen(i);
  if(SDL_JoystickOpened(i))
  {
    m_joysticks.push_back(joy);
    m_joystickValues.push_back(std::make_pair(new
    Vector2D(0,0),new Vector2D(0,0))); // add our pair
  }
  else
  {
    std::cout << SDL_GetError();
  }
}
```

We need a way to grab the values we need from this array of pairs; we will declare two new functions to the InputHandler class:

```
int xvalue(int joy, int stick);
int yvalue(int joy, int stick);
```

The joy parameter is the identifier (ID) of the joystick we want to use, and the stick is 1 for the left stick and 2 for the right stick. Let's define these functions:

```
int InputHandler::xvalue(int joy, int stick);
{
  if(m_joystickValues.size() > 0)
  {
```

Exploring Movement and Input Handling

```
    if(stick == 1)
    {
      return m_joystickValues[joy].first->getX();
    }
    else if(stick == 2)
    {
      return m_joystickValues[joy].second->getX();
    }
  }
  return 0;
}

int InputHandler::yvalue(int joy, int stick)
{
  if(m_joystickValues.size() > 0)
  {
    if(stick == 1)
    {
      return m_joystickValues[joy].first->getY();
    }
    else if(stick == 2)
    {
      return m_joystickValues[joy].second->getY();
    }
  }
  return 0;
}
```

So we grab the x or y value based on the parameters passed to each function. The `first` and `second` values are the first or second objects of the pair in the array, with `joy` being the index of the array. We can now set these values accordingly in the event loop.

```
SDL_Event event;
while(SDL_PollEvent(&event))
{
  if(event.type == SDL_QUIT)
  {
    TheGame::Instance()->quit();
  }

  if(event.type == SDL_JOYAXISMOTION)
  {
    int whichOne = event.jaxis.which;
```

```
// left stick move left or right
if(event.jaxis.axis == 0)
{
  if (event.jaxis.value > m_joystickDeadZone)
  {
    m_joystickValues[whichOne].first->setX(1);
  }
  else if(event.jaxis.value < -m_joystickDeadZone)
  {
    m_joystickValues[whichOne].first->setX(-1);
  }
  else
  {
    m_joystickValues[whichOne].first->setX(0);
  }
}

// left stick move up or down
if(event.jaxis.axis == 1)
{
  if (event.jaxis.value > m_joystickDeadZone)
  {
    m_joystickValues[whichOne].first->setY(1);
  }
  else if(event.jaxis.value < -m_joystickDeadZone)
  {
    m_joystickValues[whichOne].first->setY(-1);
  }
  else
  {
    m_joystickValues[whichOne].first->setY(0);
  }
}

// right stick move left or right
if(event.jaxis.axis == 3)
{
  if (event.jaxis.value > m_joystickDeadZone)
  {
    m_joystickValues[whichOne].second->setX(1);
  }
  else if(event.jaxis.value < -m_joystickDeadZone)
  {
    m_joystickValues[whichOne].second->setX(-1);
```

```
          }
          else
          {
            m_joystickValues[whichOne].second->setX(0);
          }
        }

        // right stick move up or down
        if(event.jaxis.axis == 4)
        {
          if (event.jaxis.value > m_joystickDeadZone)
          {
            m_joystickValues[whichOne].second->setY(1);
          }
          else if(event.jaxis.value < -m_joystickDeadZone)
          {
            m_joystickValues[whichOne].second->setY(-1);
          }
          else
          {
            m_joystickValues[whichOne].second->setY(0);
          }
        }
      }
    }
```

That is a big function! It is, however, relatively straightforward. We first check for an `SDL_JOYAXISMOTION` event and we then find out which controller the event came from using the `which` value.

```
int whichOne = event.jaxis.which;
```

From this we know which joystick the event came from and can set a value in the array accordingly; for example:

```
m_joystickValues[whichOne]
```

First we check the axis the event came from:

```
if(event.jaxis.axis == 0) // ...1,3,4
```

If the axis is 0 or 1, it is the left stick, and if it is 3 or 4, it is the right stick. We use `first` or `second` of the pair to set the left or right stick. You may also have noticed the `m_joystickDeadZone` variable. We use this to account for the sensitivity of a controller. We can set this as a constant variable in the `InputHandler` header file:

```
const int m_joystickDeadZone = 10000;
```

The value `10000` may seem like a big value to use for a stick at rest, but the sensitivity of a controller can be very high and so requires a value as large as this. Change this value accordingly for your own controllers.

Just to solidify what we are doing here, let's look closely at one scenario.

```
// left stick move left or right
{
  if (event.jaxis.value > m_joystickDeadZone)
  {
    m_joystickValues[whichOne].first->setX(1);
  }
  else if(event.jaxis.value < -m_joystickDeadZone)
  {
    m_joystickValues[whichOne].first->setX(-1);
  }
  else
  {
    m_joystickValues[whichOne].first->setX(0);
  }
}
```

If we get to the second if statement, we know that we are dealing with a left or right movement event on the left stick due to the axis being 0. We have already set which controller the event was from and adjusted `whichOne` to the correct value. We also want `first` of the pair to be the left stick. So if the axis is 0, we use the `first` object of the array and set its x value, as we are dealing with an x movement event. So why do we set the value to 1 or -1? We will answer this by starting to move our `Player` object.

Open up `Player.h` and we can start to use our `InputHandler` to get events. First we will declare a new private function:

```
private:

void handleInput();
```

Exploring Movement and Input Handling

Now in our `Player.cpp` file we can define this function to work with the `InputHandler`.

```cpp
void Player::handleInput()
{
  if(TheInputHandler::Instance()->joysticksInitialised())
  {
    if(TheInputHandler::Instance()->xvalue(0, 1) > 0 ||
    TheInputHandler::Instance()->xvalue(0, 1) < 0)
    {
      m_velocity.setX(1 * TheInputHandler::Instance()->xvalue(0,
      1));
    }
    if(TheInputHandler::Instance()->yvalue(0, 1) > 0 ||
    TheInputHandler::Instance()->yvalue(0, 1) < 0)
    {
      m_velocity.setY(1 * TheInputHandler::Instance()->yvalue(0,
      1));
    }
    if(TheInputHandler::Instance()->xvalue(0, 2) > 0 ||
    TheInputHandler::Instance()->xvalue(0, 2) < 0)
    {
      m_velocity.setX(1 * TheInputHandler::Instance()->xvalue(0,
      2));
    }
    if(TheInputHandler::Instance()->yvalue(0, 2) > 0 ||
    TheInputHandler::Instance()->yvalue(0, 2) < 0)
    {
      m_velocity.setY(1 * TheInputHandler::Instance()->yvalue(0,
      2));
    }
  }
}
```

Then we can call this function in the `Player::update` function.

```cpp
void Player::update()
{
  m_velocity.setX(0);
  m_velocity.setY(0);

  handleInput(); // add our function

  m_currentFrame = int(((SDL_GetTicks() / 100) % 6));

  SDLGameObject::update();
}
```

Everything is in place now, but first let's go through how we are setting our movement.

```
if(TheInputHandler::Instance()->xvalue(0, 1) > 0 ||
TheInputHandler::Instance()->xvalue(0, 1) < 0)
{
  m_velocity.setX(1 * TheInputHandler::Instance()->xvalue(0, 1));
}
```

Here, we first check whether xvalue of the left stick is more than 0 (that it has moved). If so, we set our Player x velocity to be the speed we want multiplied by xvalue of the left stick, and we know this is either 1 or -1. As you will know, multiplying a positive number by a negative number results in a negative number, so multiplying the speed we want by -1 will mean we are setting our x velocity to a minus value (move left). We do the same for the other stick and also the y values. Build the project and start moving your Player object with a gamepad. You could also plug in another controller and update the Enemy class to use it.

Dealing with joystick button input

Our next step is to implement a way to handle button input from our controllers. This is actually a lot simpler than handling axes. We need to know the current state of each button so that we can check whenever one has been pressed or released. To do this, we will declare an array of Boolean values, so each controller (the first index into the array) will have an array of Boolean values, one for each button on the controller.

```
std::vector<std::vector<bool>> m_buttonStates;
```

We can grab the current button state with a function that looks up the correct button from the correct joystick.

```
bool getButtonState(int joy, int buttonNumber)
{
  return m_buttonStates[joy][buttonNumber];
}
```

The first parameter is the index into the array (the joystick ID), and the second is the index into the buttons. Next we are going to have to initialize this array for each controller and each of its buttons. We will do this in the initialiseJoysticks function.

```
for(int i = 0; i < SDL_NumJoysticks(); i++)
{
  SDL_Joystick* joy = SDL_JoystickOpen(i);
  if(SDL_JoystickOpened(i))
```

Exploring Movement and Input Handling

```
  {
    m_joysticks.push_back(joy);
    m_joystickValues.push_back(std::make_pair(new
    Vector2D(0,0), new Vector2D(0,0)));

    std::vector<bool> tempButtons;

    for(int j = 0; j < SDL_JoystickNumButtons(joy); j++)
    {
      tempButtons.push_back(false);
    }

    m_buttonStates.push_back(tempButtons);
  }
}
```

We use `SDL_JoystickNumButtons` to get the number of buttons for each of our joysticks. We then push a value for each of these buttons into an array. We push `false` to start, as no buttons are pressed. This array is then pushed into our m_buttonStates array to be used with the `getButtonState` function. Now we must listen for button events and set the value in the array accordingly.

```
if(event.type == SDL_JOYBUTTONDOWN)
{
  int whichOne = event.jaxis.which;

  m_buttonStates[whichOne][event.jbutton.button] = true;
}

if(event.type == SDL_JOYBUTTONUP)
{
  int whichOne = event.jaxis.which;

  m_buttonStates[whichOne][event.jbutton.button] = false;
}
```

When a button is pressed (`SDL_JOYBUTTONDOWN`) we get to know which controller it was pressed on and use this as an index into the m_buttonStates array. We then use the button number (`event.jbutton.button`) to set the correct button to `true`; the same applies when a button is released (`SDL_JOYBUTTONUP`). That is pretty much it for button handling. Let's test it out in our Player class.

```
if(TheInputHandler::Instance()->getButtonState(0, 3))
{
  m_velocity.setX(1);
}
```

Here we are checking if button 3 has been pressed (Yellow or Y on an Xbox controller) and setting our velocity if it has. That is everything we will cover about joysticks in this book. You will realize that supporting many joysticks is very tricky and requires a lot of tweaking to ensure each one is handled correctly. However, there are ways through which you can start to have support for many joysticks; for example, through a configuration file or even by the use of inheritance for different joystick types.

Handling mouse events

Unlike joysticks, we do not have to initialize the mouse. We can also safely assume that there will only be one mouse plugged in at a time, so we will not need to handle multiple mouse devices. We can start by looking at the available mouse events that SDL covers:

SDL Mouse Event	Purpose
SDL_MouseButtonEvent	A button on the mouse has been pressed or released
SDL_MouseMotionEvent	The mouse has been moved
SDL_MouseWheelEvent	The mouse wheel has moved

Just like the joystick events, each mouse event has a type value; the following table shows each of these values:

SDL Mouse Event	Type Value
SDL_MouseButtonEvent	SDL_MOUSEBUTTONDOWN or SDL_MOUSEBUTTONUP
SDL_MouseMotionEvent	SDL_MOUSEMOTION
SDL_MouseWheelEvent	SDL_MOUSEWHEEL

We will not implement any mouse wheel movement events as most games will not use them.

Using mouse button events

Implementing mouse button events is as straightforward as joystick events, more so even as we have only three buttons to choose from: left, right, and middle. SDL numbers these as 0 for left, 1 for middle, and 2 for right. In our `InputHandler` header, let's declare a similar array to the joystick buttons, but this time a one-dimensional array, as we won't handle multiple mouse devices.

```
std::vector<bool> m_mouseButtonStates;
```

Exploring Movement and Input Handling

Then in the constructor of our `InputHandler` we can push our three mouse button states (defaulted to `false`) into the array:

```
for(int i = 0; i < 3; i++)
{
  m_mouseButtonStates.push_back(false);
}
```

Back in our header file, let's create an `enum` attribute to help us with the values of the mouse buttons. Put this above the class so that other files that include our `InputHandler.h` header can use it too.

```
enum mouse_buttons
{
    LEFT = 0,
    MIDDLE = 1,
    RIGHT = 2
};
```

Now let's handle mouse events in our event loop:

```
if(event.type == SDL_MOUSEBUTTONDOWN)
{
  if(event.button.button == SDL_BUTTON_LEFT)
  {
    m_mouseButtonStates[LEFT] = true;
  }

  if(event.button.button == SDL_BUTTON_MIDDLE)
  {
    m_mouseButtonStates[MIDDLE] = true;
  }

  if(event.button.button == SDL_BUTTON_RIGHT)
  {
    m_mouseButtonStates[RIGHT] = true;
  }
}

if(event.type == SDL_MOUSEBUTTONUP)
{
  if(event.button.button == SDL_BUTTON_LEFT)
  {
    m_mouseButtonStates[LEFT] = false;
  }
```

```
    if(event.button.button == SDL_BUTTON_MIDDLE)
    {
      m_mouseButtonStates[MIDDLE] = false;
    }

    if(event.button.button == SDL_BUTTON_RIGHT)
    {
      m_mouseButtonStates[RIGHT] = false;
    }
  }
```

We also need a function to access our mouse button states. Let's add this public function to the `InputHandler` header file:

```
bool getMouseButtonState(int buttonNumber)
{
  return m_mouseButtonStates[buttonNumber];
}
```

That is everything we need for mouse button events. We can now test it in our `Player` class.

```
if(TheInputHandler::Instance()->getMouseButtonState(LEFT))
{
  m_velocity.setX(1);
}
```

Handling mouse motion events

Mouse motion events are very important, especially in big 3D first or third person action titles. For our 2D games, we might want our character to follow the mouse as a way to control our objects, or we might want objects to move to where the mouse was clicked (for a strategy game perhaps). We may even just want to know where the mouse was clicked so that we can use it for menus. Fortunately for us, mouse motion events are relatively simple. We will start by creating a private `Vector2D*` in the header file to use as the position variable for our mouse:

```
Vector2D* m_mousePosition;
```

Next, we need a public accessor for this:

```
Vector2D* getMousePosition()
{
  return m_mousePosition;
}
```

Exploring Movement and Input Handling

And we can now handle this in our event loop:

```
if(event.type == SDL_MOUSEMOTION)
{
  m_mousePosition->setX(event.motion.x);
  m_mousePosition->setY(event.motion.y);
}
```

That is all we need for mouse motion. So let's make our `Player` function follow the mouse position to test this feature:

```
Vector2D* vec = TheInputHandler::Instance()->getMousePosition();

m_velocity = (*vec - m_position) / 100;
```

Here we have set our velocity to a vector from the player's current position to the mouse position. You can get this vector by subtracting the desired location from the current location; we already have a vector subtract overloaded operator so this is easy for us. We also divide the vector by 100; this just dampens the speed slightly so that we can see it following rather than just sticking to the mouse position. Remove the / to have your object follow the mouse exactly.

Implementing keyboard input

Our final method of input, and the simplest of the three, is keyboard input. We don't have to handle any motion events, we just want the state of each button. We aren't going to declare an array here because SDL has a built-in function that will give us an array with the state of every key; 1 being pressed and 0 not pressed.

```
SDL_GetKeyboardState(int* numkeys)
```

The `numkeys` parameter will return the number of keys available on the keyboard (the length of the `keystate` array). So in our `InputHandler` header we can declare a pointer to the array that will be returned from `SDL_GetKeyboardState`.

```
Uint8* m_keystate;
```

When we update our event handler we can also update the state of the keys; put this at the top of our event loop.

```
m_keystates = SDL_GetKeyboardState(0);
```

We will now need to create a simple function that checks whether a key is down or not.

```
bool InputHandler::isKeyDown(SDL_Scancode key)
{
  if(m_keystates != 0)
  {
    if(m_keystates[key] == 1)
    {
      return true;
    }
    else
    {
      return false;
    }
  }

  return false;
}
```

This function takes SDL_SCANCODE as a parameter. The full list of SDL_SCANCODE values can be found in the SDL documentation at http://wiki.libsdl.org/moin.cgi.

We can test the keys in our Player class. We will use the arrow keys to move our player.

```
if(TheInputHandler::Instance()->isKeyDown(SDL_SCANCODE_RIGHT))
{
  m_velocity.setX(2);
}

if(TheInputHandler::Instance()->isKeyDown(SDL_SCANCODE_LEFT))
{
  m_velocity.setX(-2);
}

if(TheInputHandler::Instance()->isKeyDown(SDL_SCANCODE_UP))
{
  m_velocity.setY(-2);
}

if(TheInputHandler::Instance()->isKeyDown(SDL_SCANCODE_DOWN))
{
  m_velocity.setY(2);
}
```

Exploring Movement and Input Handling

We now have key handling in place. Test as many keys as you can and look up the `SDL_Scancode` for the keys you are most likely to want to use.

Wrapping things up

We have now implemented all of the devices we are going to handle, but at the moment our event loop is in a bit of a mess. We need to break it up into more manageable chunks. We will do this with the use of a switch statement for event types and some private functions, within our `InputHandler`. First let's declare our functions in the header file:

```
// private functions to handle different event types

// handle keyboard events
void onKeyDown();
void onKeyUp();

// handle mouse events
void onMouseMove(SDL_Event& event);
void onMouseButtonDown(SDL_Event& event);
void onMouseButtonUp(SDL_Event& event);

// handle joysticks events
void onJoystickAxisMove(SDL_Event& event);
void onJoystickButtonDown(SDL_Event& event);
void onJoystickButtonUp(SDL_Event& event);
```

We pass in the event from the event loop into each function (apart from keys) so that we can handle them accordingly. We now need to create our switch statement in the event loop.

```
void InputHandler::update()
{
  SDL_Event event;
  while(SDL_PollEvent(&event))
  {
    switch (event.type)
    {
    case SDL_QUIT:
      TheGame::Instance()->quit();
    break;

    case SDL_JOYAXISMOTION:
      onJoystickAxisMove(event);
```

```
              break;

          case SDL_JOYBUTTONDOWN:
              onJoystickButtonDown(event);
              break;

          case SDL_JOYBUTTONUP:
              onJoystickButtonUp(event);
              break;

          case SDL_MOUSEMOTION:
              onMouseMove(event);
              break;

          case SDL_MOUSEBUTTONDOWN:
              onMouseButtonDown(event);
              break;

          case SDL_MOUSEBUTTONUP:
              onMouseButtonUp(event);
              break;

          case SDL_KEYDOWN:
              onKeyDown();
              break;

          case SDL_KEYUP:
              onKeyUp();
              break;

          default:
              break;
        }
    }
}
```

As you can see, we now break up our event loop and call the associated function depending on the type of the event. We can now split all our previous work into these functions; for example, we can put all of our mouse button down handling code into the `onMouseButtonDown` function.

```
    void InputHandler::onMouseButtonDown(SDL_Event& event)
    {
      if(event.button.button == SDL_BUTTON_LEFT)
      {
```

```
      m_mouseButtonStates[LEFT] = true;
    }

    if(event.button.button == SDL_BUTTON_MIDDLE)
    {
      m_mouseButtonStates[MIDDLE] = true;
    }

    if(event.button.button == SDL_BUTTON_RIGHT)
    {
      m_mouseButtonStates[RIGHT] = true;
    }
  }
```

The rest of the code for the `InputHandler` is available within the source code downloads.

Summary

We have covered some complicated material in this chapter. We have looked at a small amount of vector mathematics and how we can use it to move our game objects. We've also covered the initialization and the use of multiple joysticks and axes and the use of a mouse and a keyboard. Finally, we wrapped everything up with a tidy way to handle our events.

5
Handling Game States

When we first start up a game, we expect to see a splash screen showing any branding for publishers and developers, followed by a loading screen as the game does its initial setup. After this, we are usually faced with a menu screen; here, we can change settings and start the game. Starting the game leads us to another loading screen, possibly followed by a cut scene, and finally, we are in the game. When we are in the game, we can pause our play (allowing us to change any settings), exit the game, restart the level, and so on. If we fail the level, we are shown either an animation or a game over screen depending on how the game is set up. All of these different sections of a game are called *Game States*. It is very important that we make the transition between these states as easy as possible.

In this chapter we will cover:

- Two different ways of handling states, starting with a really simple implementation and gradually building our framework implementation
- Implementing **Finite State Machines (FSM)**
- Adding states to the overall framework

A simple way for switching states

One of the simplest ways to handle states is to load everything we want at the game's initialization stage, but only draw and update the objects specific to each state. Let's look at an example of how this could work. First, we can define a set of states we are going to use:

```
enum game_states
{
  MENU = 0,
  PLAY = 1,
  GAMEOVER = 2
};
```

Handling Game States

We can then use the `Game::init` function to create the objects:

```
// create menu objects
m_pMenuObj1 = new MenuObject();
m_pMenuObj1 = new MenuObject();

// create play objects
m_pPlayer = new Player();
m_pEnemy = new Enemy();

// create game over objects…
```

Then, set our initial state:

```
m_currentGameState = MENU;
```

Next, we can change our `update` function to only use the things we want when in a specific state:

```
void Game::update()
{
  switch(m_currentGameState)
  {
    case MENU:
      m_menuObj1->update();
      m_menuObj2->update();
      break;

    case PLAY:
      m_pPlayer->update();
      m_pEnemy->update();

    case GAMEOVER:
      // do game over stuff…
  }
}
```

The `render` function would do something similar. These functions could of course still loop through arrays and use polymorphism as we originally had done, but on a state-by-state basis. Changing states is as simple as changing the value of the `m_currentGameState` variable.

If you can see issues with this method, then it is very encouraging that you are starting to think in an object-oriented way. This way of updating states would be a bit of a nightmare to maintain and the scope for error is quite large. There are too many areas that need to be updated and changed to make this a viable solution for any game larger than a simple arcade game.

Implementing finite state machines

What we really need is the ability to define our states outside the `game` class, and have the state itself take care of what it needs to load, render, and update. For this we can create what is known as an FSM. The definition of FSM, as we will use it, is a machine that can exist in a finite number of states, can exist in only one state at a time (known as the current state), and can change from one state to another (known as a transition).

A base class for game states

Let's start our implementation by creating a base class for all of our states; create a header file called `GameState.h`:

```
#include<string>
class GameState
{
public:
  virtual void update() = 0;
  virtual void render() = 0;

  virtual bool onEnter() = 0;
  virtual bool onExit() = 0;

  virtual std::string getStateID() const = 0;
};
```

Just like our `GameObject` class, this is an abstract base class; we aren't actually putting any functionality into it, we just want all of our derived classes to follow this blueprint. The `update` and `render` functions are self-explanatory, as they will function just like the functions we created in the `Game` class. We can think of the `onEnter` and `onExit` functions as similar to other `load` and `clean` functions; we call the `onEnter` function as soon as a state is created and `onExit` once it is removed. The last function is a getter for the state ID; each state will need to define this function and return its own `static const` ID. The ID is used to ensure that states don't get repeated. There should be no need to change to the same state, so we check this using the state ID.

That's it for our `GameState` base class; we can now create some test states that derive from this class. We will start with a state called `MenuState`. Go ahead and create `MenuState.h` and `MenuState.cpp` in our project, open up `MenuState.h`, and start coding:

```
#include"GameState.h"

class MenuState : public GameState
{
```

Handling Game States

```cpp
public:

  virtual void update();
  virtual void render();

  virtual bool onEnter();
  virtual bool onExit();

  virtual std::string getStateID() const { return s_menuID; }

private:

  static const std::string s_menuID;
};
```

We can now define these methods in our `MenuState.cpp` file. We will just display some text in the console window for now while we test our implementation; we will give this state an ID of `"MENU"`:

```cpp
#include "MenuState.h"

const std::string MenuState::s_menuID = "MENU";

void MenuState::update()
{
  // nothing for now
}

void MenuState::render()
{
  // nothing for now
}

bool MenuState::onEnter()
{
  std::cout << "entering MenuState\n";
  return true;
}

bool MenuState::onExit()
{
  std::cout << "exiting MenuState\n";
  return true;
}
```

We will now create another state called `PlayState`, create `PlayState.h` and `PlayState.cpp` in our project, and declare our methods in the header file:

```
#include "GameState.h"

class PlayState : public GameState
{
public:

    virtual void update();
    virtual void render();

    virtual bool onEnter();
    virtual bool onExit();

    virtual std::string getStateID() const { return s_playID; }

private:

    static const std::string s_playID;
};
```

This header file is the same as `MenuState.h` with the only difference being `getStateID` returning this class' specific ID (`"PLAY"`). Let's define our functions:

```
#include "PlayState.h"

const std::string PlayState::s_playID = "PLAY";

void PlayState::update()
{
    // nothing for now
}

void PlayState::render()
{
    // nothing for now
}

bool PlayState::onEnter()
{
    std::cout << "entering PlayState\n";
    return true;
}
```

Handling Game States

```
bool PlayState::onExit()
{
  std::cout << "exiting PlayState\n";
  return true;
}
```

We now have two states ready for testing; we must next create our FSM so that we can handle them.

Implementing FSM

Our FSM is going to need to handle our states in a number of ways, which include:

- **Removing one state and adding another**: We will use this way to completely change states without leaving the option to return
- **Adding one state without removing the previous state**: This way is useful for pause menus and so on
- **Removing one state without adding another**: This way will be used to remove pause states or any other state that had been pushed on top of another one

Now that we have come up with the behavior we want our FSM to have, let's start creating the class. Create the `GameStateMachine.h` and `GameStateMachine.cpp` files in our project. We will start by declaring our functions in the header file:

```
#include "GameState.h"

class GameStateMachine
{
public:

  void pushState(GameState* pState);
  void changeState(GameState* pState);
  void popState();
};
```

We have declared the three functions we need. The `pushState` function will add a state without removing the previous state, the `changeState` function will remove the previous state before adding another, and finally, the `popState` function will remove whichever state is currently being used without adding another. We will need a place to store these states; we will use a vector:

```
private:

std::vector<GameState*> m_gameStates;
```

In the `GameStateMachine.cpp` file, we can define these functions and then go through them step-by-step:

```
void GameStateMachine::pushState(GameState *pState)
{
  m_gameStates.push_back(pState);
  m_gameStates.back()->onEnter();
}
```

This is a very straightforward function; we simply push the passed-in `pState` parameter into the `m_gameStates` array and then call its `onEnter` function:

```
void GameStateMachine::popState()
{
  if(!m_gameStates.empty())
  {
    if(m_gameStates.back()->onExit())
    {
      delete m_gamestates.back();
      m_gameStates.pop_back();
    }
  }
}
```

Another simple function is `popState`. We first check if there are actually any states available to remove, and if so, we call the `onExit` function of the current state and then remove it:

```
void GameStateMachine::changeState(GameState *pState)
{
  if(!m_gameStates.empty())
  {
    if(m_gameStates.back()->getStateID() == pState->getStateID())
    {
      return; // do nothing
    }

    if(m_gameStates.back()->onExit())
    {
      delete m_gamestates.back();
      m_gameStates.pop_back();
    }
  }

  // push back our new state
```

Handling Game States

```
    m_gameStates.push_back(pState);

    // initialise it
    m_gameStates.back()->onEnter();
}
```

Our third function is a little more complicated. First, we must check if there are already any states in the array, and if there are, we check whether their state ID is the same as the current one, and if it is, then we do nothing. If the state IDs do not match, then we remove the current state, add our new `pState`, and call its `onEnter` function. Next, we will add new `GameStateMachine` as a member of the `Game` class:

```
GameStateMachine* m_pGameStateMachine;
```

We can then use the `Game::init` function to create our state machine and add our first state:

```
m_pGameStateMachine = new GameStateMachine();
m_pGameStateMachine->changeState(new MenuState());
```

The `Game::handleEvents` function will allow us to move between our states for now:

```
void Game::handleEvents()
{
  TheInputHandler::Instance()->update();

  if(TheInputHandler::Instance()->isKeyDown(SDL_SCANCODE_RETURN))
  {
    m_pGameStateMachine->changeState(new PlayState());
  }
}
```

When we press the *Enter* key, the state will change. Test the project and you should get the following output after changing states:

```
entering MenuState
exiting MenuState
entering PlayState
```

We now have the beginnings of our FSM and can next add `update` and `render` functions to our `GameStateMachine` header file:

```
void update();
void render();
```

We can define them in our `GameStateMachine.cpp` file:

```
void GameStateMachine::update()
{
  if(!m_gameStates.empty())
  {
    m_gameStates.back()->update();
  }
}

void GameStateMachine::render()
{
  if(!m_gameStates.empty())
  {
    m_gameStates.back()->render();
  }
}
```

These functions simply check if there are any states, and if so, they update and render the current state. You will notice that we use `back()` to get the current state; this is because we have designed our FSM to always use the state at the back of the array. We use `push_back()` when adding new states so that they get pushed to the back of the array and used immediately. Our `Game` class will now use the FSM functions in place of its own `update` and `render` functions:

```
void Game::render()
{
  SDL_RenderClear(m_pRenderer);

  m_pGameStateMachine->render();

  SDL_RenderPresent(m_pRenderer);
}

void Game::update()
{
  m_pGameStateMachine->update();
}
```

Our FSM is now in place.

Implementing menu states

We will now move on to creating a simple menu state with visuals and mouse handling. We will use two new screenshots for our buttons, which are available with the source code downloads:

The following screenshot shows the exit feature:

These are essentially sprite sheets with the three states of our button. Let's create a new class for these buttons, which we will call `MenuButton`. Go ahead and create `MenuButton.h` and `MenuButton.cpp`. We will start with the header file:

```
class MenuButton : public SDLGameObject
{
public:

  MenuButton(const LoaderParams* pParams);

  virtual void draw();
  virtual void update();
  virtual void clean();
};
```

By now this should look very familiar and it should feel straightforward to create new types. We will also define our button states as an enumerated type so that our code becomes more readable; put this in the header file under `private`:

```
enum button_state
{
  MOUSE_OUT = 0,
  MOUSE_OVER = 1,
  CLICKED = 2
};
```

Open up the `MenuButton.cpp` file and we can start to flesh out our `MenuButton` class:

```
MenuButton::MenuButton(const LoaderParams* pParams) :
SDLGameObject(pParams)
{
  m_currentFrame = MOUSE_OUT; // start at frame 0
```

```
}

void MenuButton::draw()
{
  SDLGameObject::draw(); // use the base class drawing
}

void MenuButton::update()
{
  Vector2D* pMousePos = TheInputHandler::Instance()
  ->getMousePosition();

  if(pMousePos->getX() < (m_position.getX() + m_width)
  && pMousePos->getX() > m_position.getX()
  && pMousePos->getY() < (m_position.getY() + m_height)
  && pMousePos->getY() > m_position.getY())
  {
    m_currentFrame = MOUSE_OVER;

    if(TheInputHandler::Instance()->getMouseButtonState(LEFT))
    {
      m_currentFrame = CLICKED;
    }
  }
  else
  {
    m_currentFrame = MOUSE_OUT;
  }
}

void MenuButton::clean()
{
  SDLGameObject::clean();
}
```

The only thing really new in this class is the `update` function. Next, we will go through each step of this function:

- First, we get the coordinates of the mouse pointer and store them in a pointer to a `Vector2D` object:

    ```
    Vector2D* pMousePos = TheInputHandler::Instance()-
    >getMousePosition();
    ```

Handling Game States

- Now, check whether the mouse is over the button or not. We do this by first checking whether the mouse position is less than the position of the right-hand side of the button (*x position + width*). We then check if the mouse position is greater than the position of the left-hand side of the button (*x position*). The y-position check is essentially the same with *y position + height* and *y position* for bottom and top respectively:

  ```
  if(pMousePos->getX() < (m_position.getX() + m_width)
  && pMousePos->getX() > m_position.getX()
  && pMousePos->getY() < (m_position.getY() + m_height)
  && pMousePos->getY() > m_position.getY())
  ```

- If the previous check is true, we know that the mouse is hovering over our button; we set its frame to MOUSE_OVER (1):

  ```
  m_currentFrame = MOUSE_OVER;
  ```

- We can then check whether the mouse has been clicked; if it has, then we set the current frame to CLICKED (2):

  ```
  if(TheInputHandler::Instance()->getMouseButtonState(LEFT))
  {
    m_currentFrame = CLICKED;
  }
  ```

- If the check is not true, then we know the mouse is outside the button and we set the frame to MOUSE_OUT (0):

  ```
  else
  {
    m_currentFrame = MOUSE_OUT;
  }
  ```

We can now test out our reusable button class. Open up our previously created `MenuState.hand`, which we will implement for real. First, we are going to need a vector of `GameObject*` to store our menu items:

```
std::vector<GameObject*> m_gameObjects;
```

Inside the `MenuState.cpp` file, we can now start handling our menu items:

```
void MenuState::update()
{
  for(int i = 0; i < m_gameObjects.size(); i++)
  {
    m_gameObjects[i]->update();
  }
}
```

```
void MenuState::render()
{
  for(int i = 0; i < m_gameObjects.size(); i++)
  {
    m_gameObjects[i]->draw();
  }
}
```

The onExit and onEnter functions can be defined as follows:

```
bool MenuState::onEnter()
{
  if(!TheTextureManager::Instance()->load("assets/button.png",
  "playbutton", TheGame::Instance()->getRenderer()))
  {
    return false;
  }

  if(!TheTextureManager::Instance()->load("assets/exit.png",
  "exitbutton", TheGame::Instance()->getRenderer()))
  {
    return false;
  }

  GameObject* button1 = new MenuButton(new LoaderParams(100, 100,
  400, 100, "playbutton"));
  GameObject* button2 = new MenuButton(new LoaderParams(100, 300,
  400, 100, "exitbutton"));

  m_gameObjects.push_back(button1);
  m_gameObjects.push_back(button2);

  std::cout << "entering MenuState\n";
  return true;
}

bool MenuState::onExit()
{
  for(int i = 0; i < m_gameObjects.size(); i++)
  {
    m_gameObjects[i]->clean();
  }
  m_gameObjects.clear();
  TheTextureManager::Instance()
  ->clearFromTextureMap("playbutton");
  TheTextureManager::Instance()
```

[113]

```
     ->clearFromTextureMap("exitbutton");

    std::cout << "exiting MenuState\n";
    return true;
}
```

We use `TextureManager` to load our new images and then assign these textures to two buttons. The `TextureManager` class also has a new function called `clearFromTextureMap`, which takes the ID of the texture we want to remove; it is defined as follows:

```
void TextureManager::clearFromTextureMap(std::string id)
{
  m_textureMap.erase(id);
}
```

This function enables us to clear only the textures from the current state, not the entire texture map. This is essential when we push states and then pop them, as we do not want the popped state to clear the original state's textures.

Everything else is essentially identical to how we handle objects in the `Game` class. Run the project and we will have buttons that react to mouse events. The window will look like the following screenshot (go ahead and test it out):

Function pointers and callback functions

Our buttons react to rollovers and clicks but do not actually do anything yet. What we really want to achieve is the ability to create `MenuButton` and pass in the function we want it to call once it is clicked; we can achieve this through the use of function pointers. Function pointers do exactly as they say: they point to a function. We can use classic C style function pointers for the moment, as we are only going to use functions that do not take any parameters and always have a return type of `void` (therefore, we do not need to make them generic at this point).

The syntax for a function pointer is like this:

```
returnType (*functionName)(parameters);
```

We declare our function pointer as a private member in `MenuButton.h` as follows:

```
void (*m_callback)();
```

We also add a new member variable to handle clicking better:

```
bool m_bReleased;
```

Now we can alter the constructor to allow us to pass in our function:

```
MenuButton(const LoaderParams* pParams, void (*callback)());
```

In our `MenuButton.cpp` file, we can now alter the constructor and initialize our pointer with the initialization list:

```
MenuButton::MenuButton(const LoaderParams* pParams, void (*callback)()
) : SDLGameObject(pParams), m_callback(callback)
```

The `update` function can now call this function:

```
void MenuButton::update()
{
  Vector2D* pMousePos = TheInputHandler::Instance()
  ->getMousePosition();

  if(pMousePos->getX() < (m_position.getX() + m_width)
  && pMousePos->getX() > m_position.getX()
  && pMousePos->getY() < (m_position.getY() + m_height)
  && pMousePos->getY() > m_position.getY())
  {
    if(TheInputHandler::Instance()->getMouseButtonState(LEFT)
    && m_bReleased)
    {
      m_currentFrame = CLICKED;

      m_callback(); // call our callback function

      m_bReleased = false;
    }
    else if(!TheInputHandler::Instance()
    ->getMouseButtonState(LEFT))
    {
      m_bReleased = true;
      m_currentFrame = MOUSE_OVER;
    }
  }
```

Handling Game States

```
    else
    {
      m_currentFrame = MOUSE_OUT;
    }
}
```

Note that this `update` function now uses the `m_bReleased` value to ensure we release the mouse button before doing the callback again; this is how we want our clicking to behave.

In our `MenuState.h` object, we can declare some functions that we will pass into the constructors of our `MenuButton` objects:

```
private:
// call back functions for menu items
static void s_menuToPlay();
static void s_exitFromMenu();
```

We have declared these functions as static; this is because our callback functionality will only support static functions. It is a little more complicated to handle regular member functions as function pointers, so we will avoid this and stick to static functions. We can define these functions in the `MenuState.cpp` file:

```
void MenuState::s_menuToPlay()
{
  std::cout << "Play button clicked\n";
}

void MenuState::s_exitFromMenu()
{
  std::cout << "Exit button clicked\n";
}
```

We can pass these functions into the constructors of our buttons:

```
GameObject* button1 = new MenuButton(new LoaderParams(100, 100, 400, 
100, "playbutton"), s_menuToPlay);
GameObject* button2 = new MenuButton(new LoaderParams(100, 300, 400, 
100, "exitbutton"), s_exitFromMenu);
```

Test our project and you will see our functions printing to the console. We are now passing in the function we want our button to call once it is clicked; this functionality is great for our buttons. Let's test the exit button with some real functionality:

```
void MenuState::s_exitFromMenu()
{
  TheGame::Instance()->quit();
}
```

Now clicking on our exit button will exit the game. The next step is to allow the `s_menuToPlay` function to move to `PlayState`. We first need to add a getter to the `Game.h` file to allow us to access the state machine:

```
GameStateMachine* getStateMachine(){ return m_pGameStateMachine; }
```

We can now use this to change states in `MenuState`:

```
void MenuState::s_menuToPlay()
{
  TheGame::Instance()->getStateMachine()->changeState(new
  PlayState());
}
```

Go ahead and test; `PlayState` does not do anything yet, but our console output should show the movement between states.

Implementing the temporary play state

We have created `MenuState`; next, we need to create `PlayState` so that we can visually see the change in our states. For `PlayState` we will create a player object that uses our `helicopter.png` image and follows the mouse around. We will start with the `Player.cpp` file and add the code to make the `Player` object follow the mouse position:

```
void Player::handleInput()
{
  Vector2D* target = TheInputHandler::Instance()
  ->getMousePosition();

  m_velocity = *target - m_position;

  m_velocity /= 50;
}
```

First, we get the current mouse location; we can then get a vector that leads from the current position to the mouse position by subtracting the current position from the mouse position. We then divide the velocity by a scalar to slow us down a little and allow us to see our helicopter catch up to the mouse rather than stick to it. Our `PlayState.h` file will now need its own vector of `GameObject*`:

```
class GameObject;

class PlayState : public GameState
{
public:
```

Handling Game States

```cpp
    virtual void update();
    virtual void render();

    virtual bool onEnter();
    virtual bool onExit();

    virtual std::string getStateID() const { return s_playID; }

  private:

    static const std::string s_playID;

    std::vector<GameObject*> m_gameObjects;
};
```

Finally, we must update the `PlayState.cpp` implementation file to use our `Player` object:

```cpp
    const std::string PlayState::s_playID = "PLAY";

    void PlayState::update()
    {
      for(int i = 0; i < m_gameObjects.size(); i++)
      {
        m_gameObjects[i]->update();
      }
    }

    void PlayState::render()
    {
      for(int i = 0; i < m_gameObjects.size(); i++)
      {
        m_gameObjects[i]->draw();
      }
    }

    bool PlayState::onEnter()
    {
      if(!TheTextureManager::Instance()->load("assets/helicopter.png",
      "helicopter", TheGame::Instance()->getRenderer()))
      {
        return false;
      }
```

```
    GameObject* player = new Player(new LoaderParams(100, 100, 128,
    55, "helicopter"));

    m_gameObjects.push_back(player);

    std::cout << "entering PlayState\n";
    return true;
}

bool PlayState::onExit()
{
    for(int i = 0; i < m_gameObjects.size(); i++)
    {
        m_gameObjects[i]->clean();
    }
    m_gameObjects.clear();
    TheTextureManager::Instance()
    ->clearFromTextureMap("helicopter");

    std::cout << "exiting PlayState\n";
    return true;
}
```

This file is very similar to the `MenuState.cpp` file, but this time we are using a `Player` object rather than the two `MenuButton` objects. There is one adjustment to our `SDLGameObject.cpp` file that will make `PlayState` look even better; we are going to flip the image file depending on the velocity of the object:

```
    void SDLGameObject::draw()
    {
        if(m_velocity.getX() > 0)
        {
            TextureManager::Instance()->drawFrame(m_textureID,
            (Uint32)m_position.getX(), (Uint32)m_position.getY(),
            m_width, m_height, m_currentRow, m_currentFrame,
            TheGame::Instance()->getRenderer(),SDL_FLIP_HORIZONTAL);
        }
        else
        {
            TextureManager::Instance()->drawFrame(m_textureID,
            (Uint32)m_position.getX(), (Uint32)m_position.getY(),
            m_width, m_height, m_currentRow, m_currentFrame,
            TheGame::Instance()->getRenderer());
        }
    }
```

Handling Game States

We check whether the object's velocity is more than 0 (moving to the right-hand side) and flip the image accordingly. Run our game and you will now have the ability to move between `MenuState` and `PlayState` each with their own functionality and objects. The following screenshot shows our project so far:

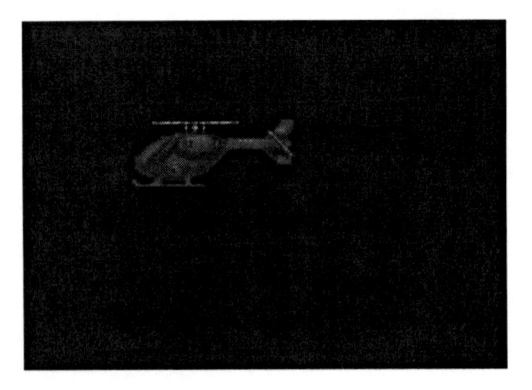

Pausing the game

Another very important state for our games is the pause state. Once paused, the game could have all kinds of options. Our `PauseState` class will be very similar to the `MenuState`, but with different button visuals and callbacks. Here are our two new screenshots (again available in the source code download):

The following screenshot shows the resume functionality:

Let's start by creating our `PauseState.h` file in the project:

```
class GameObject;

class PauseState : public GameState
{
public:

    virtual void update();
```

```
    virtual void render();

    virtual bool onEnter();
    virtual bool onExit();

    virtual std::string getStateID() const { return s_pauseID; }

  private:

    static void s_pauseToMain();
    static void s_resumePlay();

    static const std::string s_pauseID;

    std::vector<GameObject*> m_gameObjects;
};
```

Next, create our `PauseState.cpp` file:

```
const std::string PauseState::s_pauseID = "PAUSE";

void PauseState::s_pauseToMain()
{
  TheGame::Instance()->getStateMachine()->changeState(new
  MenuState());
}

void PauseState::s_resumePlay()
{
  TheGame::Instance()->getStateMachine()->popState();
}

void PauseState::update()
{
  for(int i = 0; i < m_gameObjects.size(); i++)
  {
    m_gameObjects[i]->update();
  }
}

void PauseState::render()
{
  for(int i = 0; i < m_gameObjects.size(); i++)
  {
    m_gameObjects[i]->draw();
```

Handling Game States

```cpp
    }
}

bool PauseState::onEnter()
{
  if(!TheTextureManager::Instance()->load("assets/resume.png",
  "resumebutton", TheGame::Instance()->getRenderer()))
  {
    return false;
  }

  if(!TheTextureManager::Instance()->load("assets/main.png",
  "mainbutton", TheGame::Instance()->getRenderer()))
  {
    return false;
  }

  GameObject* button1 = new MenuButton(new LoaderParams(200, 100,
  200, 80, "mainbutton"), s_pauseToMain);
  GameObject* button2 = new MenuButton(new LoaderParams(200, 300,
  200, 80, "resumebutton"), s_resumePlay);

  m_gameObjects.push_back(button1);
  m_gameObjects.push_back(button2);

  std::cout << "entering PauseState\n";
  return true;
}

bool PauseState::onExit()
{
  for(int i = 0; i < m_gameObjects.size(); i++)
  {
    m_gameObjects[i]->clean();
  }
  m_gameObjects.clear();
  TheTextureManager::Instance()
  ->clearFromTextureMap("resumebutton");
  TheTextureManager::Instance()
  ->clearFromTextureMap("mainbutton");
  // reset the mouse button states to false
  TheInputHandler::Instance()->reset();

  std::cout << "exiting PauseState\n";
  return true;
}
```

In our `PlayState.cpp` file, we can now use our new `PauseState` class:

```
void PlayState::update()
{
  if(TheInputHandler::Instance()->isKeyDown(SDL_SCANCODE_ESCAPE))
  {
    TheGame::Instance()->getStateMachine()->pushState(new
    PauseState());
  }

  for(int i = 0; i < m_gameObjects.size(); i++)
  {
    m_gameObjects[i]->update();
  }
}
```

This function listens for the *Esc* key being pressed, and once it has been pressed, it then pushes a new `PauseState` class onto the state array in FSM. Remember that `pushState` does not remove the old state; it merely stops using it and uses the new state. Once we are done with the pushed state, we remove it from the state array and the game continues to use the previous state. We remove the pause state using the resume button's callback:

```
void PauseState::s_resumePlay()
{
  TheGame::Instance()->getStateMachine()->popState();
}
```

The main menu button takes us back to the main menu and completely removes any other states:

```
void PauseState::s_pauseToMain()
{
  TheGame::Instance()->getStateMachine()->changeState(new
  MenuState());
}
```

Creating the game over state

We are going to create one final state, `GameOverState`. To get to this state, we will use collision detection and a new `Enemy` object in the `PlayState` class. We will check whether the `Player` object has hit the `Enemy` object, and if so, we will change to our `GameOverState` class. Our Enemy object will use a new image `helicopter2.png`:

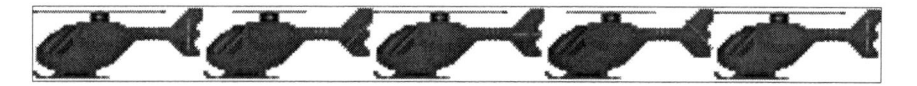

Handling Game States

We will make our `Enemy` object's helicopter move up and down the screen just to keep things interesting. In our `Enemy.cpp` file, we will add this functionality:

```cpp
Enemy::Enemy(const LoaderParams* pParams) : SDLGameObject(pParams)
{
  m_velocity.setY(2);
  m_velocity.setX(0.001);
}

void Enemy::draw()
{
  SDLGameObject::draw();
}

void Enemy::update()
{
  m_currentFrame = int(((SDL_GetTicks() / 100) % m_numFrames));

  if(m_position.getY() < 0)
  {
    m_velocity.setY(2);
  }
  else if(m_position.getY() > 400)
  {
    m_velocity.setY(-2);
  }

  SDLGameObject::update();
}
```

We can now add an `Enemy` object to our `PlayState` class:

```cpp
bool PlayState::onEnter()
{
  if(!TheTextureManager::Instance()->load("assets/helicopter.png",
  "helicopter", TheGame::Instance()->getRenderer()))
  {
    return false;
  }

  if(!TheTextureManager::Instance()
  ->load("assets/helicopter2.png", "helicopter2",
  TheGame::Instance()->getRenderer()))
  {
    return false;
```

```
    }

    GameObject* player = new Player(new LoaderParams(500, 100, 128,
    55, "helicopter"));
    GameObject* enemy = new Enemy(new LoaderParams(100, 100, 128,
    55, "helicopter2"));

    m_gameObjects.push_back(player);
    m_gameObjects.push_back(enemy);

    std::cout << "entering PlayState\n";
    return true;
}
```

Running the game will allow us to see our two helicopters:

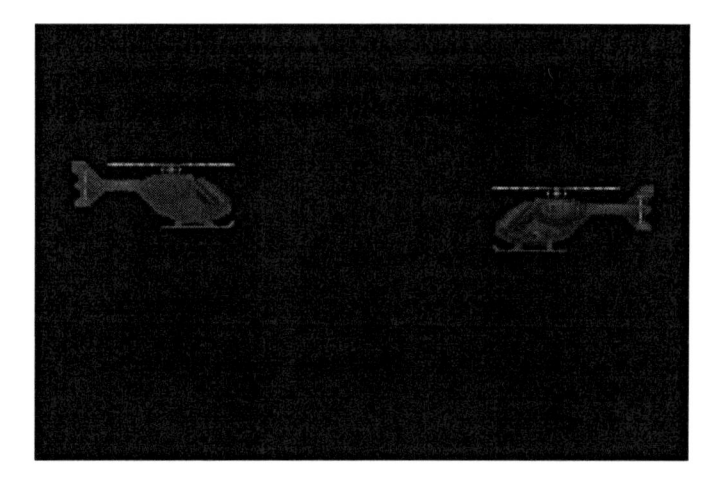

Before we cover collision detection, we are going to create our `GameOverState` class. We will be using two new images for this state, one for new `MenuButton` and one for a new type, which we will call `AnimatedGraphic`:

The following screenshot shows the game over functionality:

Handling Game States

`AnimatedGraphic` is very similar to other types, so I will not go into too much detail here; however, what is important is the added value in the constructor that controls the speed of the animation, which sets the private member variable `m_animSpeed`:

```
AnimatedGraphic::AnimatedGraphic(const LoaderParams* pParams, int
animSpeed) : SDLGameObject(pParams), m_animSpeed(animSpeed)
{

}
```

The `update` function will use this value to set the speed of the animation:

```
void AnimatedGraphic::update()
{
  m_currentFrame = int(((SDL_GetTicks() / (1000 / m_animSpeed)) %
  m_numFrames));
}
```

Now that we have the `AnimatedGraphic` class, we can implement our `GameOverState` class. Create `GameOverState.h` and `GameOverState.cpp` in our project; the header file we will create should look very familiar, as given in the following code:

```
class GameObject;

class GameOverState : public GameState
{
public:

  virtual void update();
  virtual void render();

  virtual bool onEnter();
  virtual bool onExit();

  virtual std::string getStateID() const {return s_gameOverID;}

private:

  static void s_gameOverToMain();
  static void s_restartPlay();

  static const std::string s_gameOverID;

  std::vector<GameObject*> m_gameObjects;
};
```

Our implementation file is also very similar to other files already covered, so again I will only cover the parts that are different. First, we define our static variables and functions:

```
const std::string GameOverState::s_gameOverID = "GAMEOVER";

void GameOverState::s_gameOverToMain()
{
  TheGame::Instance()->getStateMachine()->changeState(new
  MenuState());
}

void GameOverState::s_restartPlay()
{
  TheGame::Instance()->getStateMachine()->changeState(new
  PlayState());
}
```

The `onEnter` function will create three new objects along with their textures:

```
bool GameOverState::onEnter()
{
  if(!TheTextureManager::Instance()->load("assets/gameover.png",
  "gameovertext", TheGame::Instance()->getRenderer()))
  {
    return false;
  }

  if(!TheTextureManager::Instance()->load("assets/main.png",
  "mainbutton", TheGame::Instance()->getRenderer()))
  {
    return false;
  }

  if(!TheTextureManager::Instance()->load("assets/restart.png",
  "restartbutton", TheGame::Instance()->getRenderer()))
  {
    return false;
  }

  GameObject* gameOverText = new AnimatedGraphic(new
  LoaderParams(200, 100, 190, 30, "gameovertext", 2), 2);
  GameObject* button1 = new MenuButton(new LoaderParams(200, 200,
  200, 80, "mainbutton"), s_gameOverToMain);
  GameObject* button2 = new MenuButton(new LoaderParams(200, 300,
  200, 80, "restartbutton"), s_restartPlay);

  m_gameObjects.push_back(gameOverText);
```

Handling Game States

```
    m_gameObjects.push_back(button1);
    m_gameObjects.push_back(button2);

    std::cout << "entering PauseState\n";
    return true;
}
```

That is pretty much it for our `GameOverState` class, but we must now create a condition that creates this state. Move to our `PlayState.h` file and we will create a new function to allow us to check for collisions:

```
bool checkCollision(SDLGameObject* p1, SDLGameObject* p2);
```

We will define this function in `PlayState.cpp`:

```
bool PlayState::checkCollision(SDLGameObject* p1, SDLGameObject* p2)
{
    int leftA, leftB;
    int rightA, rightB;
    int topA, topB;
    int bottomA, bottomB;

    leftA = p1->getPosition().getX();
    rightA = p1->getPosition().getX() + p1->getWidth();
    topA = p1->getPosition().getY();
    bottomA = p1->getPosition().getY() + p1->getHeight();

    //Calculate the sides of rect B
    leftB = p2->getPosition().getX();
    rightB = p2->getPosition().getX() + p2->getWidth();
    topB = p2->getPosition().getY();
    bottomB = p2->getPosition().getY() + p2->getHeight();

    //If any of the sides from A are outside of B
    if( bottomA <= topB ){return false;}
    if( topA >= bottomB ){return false; }
    if( rightA <= leftB ){return false; }
    if( leftA >= rightB ){return false;}

    return true;
}
```

This function checks for collisions between two `SDLGameObject` types. For the function to work, we need to add three new functions to our `SDLGameObject` class:

```
Vector2D& getPosition() { return m_position; }
int getWidth() { return m_width; }
int getHeight() { return m_height; }
```

The next chapter will deal with how this function works, but for now, it is enough to know that it does. Our `PlayState` class will now utilize this collision detection in its `update` function:

```
void PlayState::update()
{
  if(TheInputHandler::Instance()->isKeyDown(SDL_SCANCODE_ESCAPE))
  {
    TheGame::Instance()->getStateMachine()->pushState(new
    PauseState());
  }

  for(int i = 0; i < m_gameObjects.size(); i++)
  {
    m_gameObjects[i]->update();
  }

  if(checkCollision(dynamic_cast<SDLGameObject*>
  (m_gameObjects[0]), dynamic_cast<SDLGameObject*>
  (m_gameObjects[1])))
  {
    TheGame::Instance()->getStateMachine()->pushState(new
    GameOverState());
  }
}
```

We have to use a `dynamic_cast` object to cast our `GameObject*` class to an `SDLGameObject*` class. If `checkCollision` returns `true`, then we add the `GameOverState` class. The following screenshot shows the `GameOver` state:

Summary

This chapter has left us with something a lot more like a game than in previous chapters. We have created states for menus, pause, play, and game over with each state having its own functionality and being handled using FSM. The Game class now uses FSM to render and update game objects and it does not now handle objects directly, as each individual state handles its own objects. We have also created simple callback functions for our buttons using function pointers and static functions.

6
Data-driven Design

With the previous chapter adding the ability to create and handle game states, our framework has really begun to take shape. In this chapter, we will explore a new way to create our states and objects by removing the need to hardcode the creation of our objects at compile time. To do this we will parse through an external file, in our case an XML file, which lists all of the objects needed for our state. This will make our states generic as they can be completely different simply by loading up an alternate XML file. Taking `PlayState` as an example, when creating a new level we would need to create a new state with different objects and set up objects we want for that level. If we could instead load the objects from an external file, we could reuse the same `PlayState` and simply load the correct file depending on the current level we want. Keeping classes generic like this and loading external data to determine their state is called **Data-driven Design**.

In this chapter we will cover:

- Loading XML files using the **TinyXML** library
- Creating a **Distributed Factory**
- Loading objects dynamically using the factory and an XML file
- Parsing a state from an XML file
- Fitting everything together into the framework

Loading XML files

I have chosen to use XML files because they are so easy to parse. We are not going to write our own XML parser, rather we will use an open source library called TinyXML. TinyXML was written by *Lee Thomason* and is available under the zlib license from `http://sourceforge.net/projects/tinyxml/`.

Once downloaded the only setup we need to do is to include a few of the files in our project:

- `tinyxmlerror.cpp`
- `tinyxmlparser.cpp`
- `tinystr.cpp`
- `tinystr.h`
- `tinyxml.cpp`
- `tinyxml.h`

Also, at the top of `tinyxml.h`, add this line of code:

```
#define TIXML_USE_STL
```

By doing this we ensure that we are using the STL versions of the TinyXML functions. We can now go through a little of how an XML file is structured. It's actually fairly simple and we will only give a brief overview to help you get up to speed with how we will use it.

Basic XML structure

Here is a basic XML file:

```
<?xml version="1.0" ?>
<ROOT>
    <ELEMENT>
    </ELEMENT>
</ROOT>
```

The first line of the file defines the format of the XML file. The second line is our `Root` element; everything else is a child of this element. The third line is the first child of the root element. Now let's look at a slightly more complicated XML file:

```
<?xml version="1.0" ?>
<ROOT>
    <ELEMENTS>
        <ELEMENT>Hello,</ELEMENT>
        <ELEMENT> World!</ELEMENT>
    </ELEMENTS>
</ROOT>
```

As you can see we have now added children to the first child element. You can nest as many children as you like. But without a good structure, your XML file may become very hard to read. If we were to parse the above file, here are the steps we would take:

1. Load the XML file.
2. Get the root element, `<ROOT>`.
3. Get the first child of the root element, `<ELEMENTS>`.
4. For each child, `<ELEMENT>` of `<ELEMENTS>`, get the content.
5. Close the file.

Another useful XML feature is the use of attributes. Here is an example:

```xml
<ROOT>
    <ELEMENTS>
        <ELEMENT text="Hello,"/>
        <ELEMENT text=" World!"/>
    </ELEMENTS>
</ROOT>
```

We have now stored the text we want in an attribute named `text`. When this file is parsed, we would now grab the `text` attribute for each element and store that instead of the content between the `<ELEMENT></ELEMENT>` tags. This is especially useful for us as we can use attributes to store lots of different values for our objects. So let's look at something closer to what we will use in our game:

```xml
<?xml version="1.0" ?>
<STATES>

<!--The Menu State-->
<MENU>
<TEXTURES>
  <texture filename="button.png" ID="playbutton"/>
  <texture filename="exit.png" ID="exitbutton"/>
</TEXTURES>

<OBJECTS>
  <object type="MenuButton" x="100" y="100" width="400"
  height="100" textureID="playbutton"/>
  <object type="MenuButton" x="100" y="300" width="400"
  height="100" textureID="exitbutton"/>
</OBJECTS>
</MENU>
```

```xml
<!--The Play State-->
<PLAY>
</PLAY>

<!-- The Game Over State -->
<GAMEOVER>
</GAMEOVER>
</STATES>
```

This is slightly more complex. We define each state in its own element and within this element we have objects and textures with various attributes. These attributes can be loaded in to create the state.

With this knowledge of XML you can easily create your own file structures if what we cover within this book is not to your needs.

Implementing Object Factories

We are now armed with a little XML knowledge but before we move forward, we are going to take a look at Object Factories. An object factory is a class that is tasked with the creation of our objects. Essentially, we tell the factory the object we would like it to create and it goes ahead and creates a new instance of that object and then returns it. We can start by looking at a rudimentary implementation:

```
GameObject* GameObjectFactory::createGameObject(ID id)
{
  switch(id)
  {
    case "PLAYER":
      return new Player();
    break;

    case "ENEMY":
      return new Enemy();
    break;

    // lots more object types
  }
}
```

This function is very simple. We pass in an ID for the object and the factory uses a big switch statement to look it up and return the correct object. Not a terrible solution but also not a particularly good one, as the factory will need to know about each type it needs to create and maintaining the switch statement for many different objects would be extremely tedious. Just as when we covered looping through game objects in *Chapter 3, Working with Game Objects*, we want this factory not to care about which type we ask for. It shouldn't need to know all of the specific types we want it to create. Luckily this is something that we can definitely achieve.

Using Distributed Factories

Through the use of Distributed Factories we can make a generic object factory that will create any of our types. Distributed factories allow us to dynamically maintain the types of objects we want our factory to create, rather than hard code them into a function (like in the preceding simple example). The approach we will take is to have the factory contain std::map that maps a string (the type of our object) to a small class called Creator whose only purpose is the creation of a specific object. We will register a new type with the factory using a function that takes a string (the ID) and a Creator class and adds them to the factory's map. We are going to start with the base class for all the Creator types. Create GameObjectFactory.h and declare this class at the top of the file.

```
#include <string>
#include <map>
#include "GameObject.h"

class BaseCreator
{
  public:

  virtual GameObject* createGameObject() const = 0;
  virtual ~BaseCreator() {}
};
```

We can now go ahead and create the rest of our factory and then go through it piece by piece.

```
class GameObjectFactory
{
  public:

  bool registerType(std::string typeID, BaseCreator* pCreator)
  {
    std::map<std::string, BaseCreator*>::iterator it =
```

Data-driven Design

```cpp
      m_creators.find(typeID);

      // if the type is already registered, do nothing
      if(it != m_creators.end())
      {
        delete pCreator;
        return false;
      }

      m_creators[typeID] = pCreator;

      return true;
    }

    GameObject* create(std::string typeID)
    {
      std::map<std::string, BaseCreator*>::iterator it =
      m_creators.find(typeID);

      if(it == m_creators.end())
      {
        std::cout << "could not find type: " << typeID << "\n";
        return NULL;
      }

      BaseCreator* pCreator = (*it).second;
      return pCreator->createGameObject();
    }

    private:

    std::map<std::string, BaseCreator*> m_creators;

};
```

This is quite a small class but it is actually very powerful. We will cover each part separately starting with `std::map m_creators`.

```cpp
    std::map<std::string, BaseCreator*> m_creators;
```

This map holds the important elements of our factory, the functions of the class essentially either add or remove from this map. This becomes apparent when we look at the `registerType` function:

```cpp
    bool registerType(std::string typeID, BaseCreator* pCreator)
```

[136]

This function takes the ID we want to associate the object type with (as a string), and the creator object for that class. The function then attempts to find the type using the `std::mapfind` function:

```
std::map<std::string, BaseCreator*>::iterator it =
m_creators.find(typeID);
```

If the type is found then it is already registered. The function then deletes the passed in pointer and returns `false`:

```
if(it != m_creators.end())
{
  delete pCreator;
  return false;
}
```

If the type is not already registered then it can be assigned to the map and then `true` is returned:

```
m_creators[typeID] = pCreator;
return true;
}
```

As you can see, the `registerType` function is actually very simple; it is just a way to add types to the map. The `create` function is very similar:

```
GameObject* create(std::string typeID)
{
  std::map<std::string, BaseCreator*>::iterator it =
  m_creators.find(typeID);

  if(it == m_creators.end())
  {
    std::cout << "could not find type: " << typeID << "\n";
    return 0;
  }

  BaseCreator* pCreator = (*it).second;
  return pCreator->createGameObject();
}
```

The function looks for the type in the same way as `registerType` does, but this time it checks whether the type was not found (as opposed to found). If the type is not found we return `0`, and if the type is found then we use the `Creator` object for that type to return a new instance of it as a pointer to `GameObject`.

Data-driven Design

It is worth noting that the `GameObjectFactory` class should probably be a singleton. We won't cover how to make it a singleton as this has been covered in the previous chapters. Try implementing it yourself or see how it is implemented in the source code download.

Fitting the factory into the framework

With our factory now in place, we can start altering our `GameObject` classes to use it. Our first step is to ensure that we have a `Creator` class for each of our objects. Here is one for `Player`:

```cpp
class PlayerCreator : public BaseCreator
{
  GameObject* createGameObject() const
  {
    return new Player();
  }
};
```

This can be added to the bottom of the `Player.h` file. Any object we want the factory to create must have its own `Creator` implementation. Another addition we must make is to move `LoaderParams` from the constructor to their own function called `load`. This stops the need for us to pass the `LoaderParams` object to the factory itself. We will put the `load` function into the `GameObject` base class, as we want every object to have one.

```cpp
class GameObject
{
  public:

  virtual void draw()=0;
  virtual void update()=0;
  virtual void clean()=0;

  // new load function
  virtual void load(const LoaderParams* pParams)=0;

  protected:

  GameObject() {}
  virtual ~GameObject() {}
};
```

Each of our derived classes will now need to implement this `load` function. The `SDLGameObject` class will now look like this:

```
SDLGameObject::SDLGameObject() : GameObject()
{
}

voidSDLGameObject::load(const LoaderParams *pParams)
{
  m_position = Vector2D(pParams->getX(),pParams->getY());
  m_velocity = Vector2D(0,0);
  m_acceleration = Vector2D(0,0);
  m_width = pParams->getWidth();
  m_height = pParams->getHeight();
  m_textureID = pParams->getTextureID();
  m_currentRow = 1;
  m_currentFrame = 1;
  m_numFrames = pParams->getNumFrames();
}
```

Our objects that derive from `SDLGameObject` can use this `load` function as well; for example, here is the `Player::load` function:

```
Player::Player() : SDLGameObject()
{

}

void Player::load(const LoaderParams *pParams)
{
  SDLGameObject::load(pParams);
}
```

This may seem a bit pointless but it actually saves us having to pass through `LoaderParams` everywhere. Without it, we would need to pass `LoaderParams` through the factory's `create` function which would then in turn pass it through to the `Creator` object. We have eliminated the need for this by having a specific function that handles parsing our loading values. This will make more sense once we start parsing our states from a file.

Data-driven Design

We have another issue which needs rectifying; we have two classes with extra parameters in their constructors (`MenuButton` and `AnimatedGraphic`). Both classes take an extra parameter as well as `LoaderParams`. To combat this we will add these values to `LoaderParams` and give them default values.

```
LoaderParams(int x, int y, int width, int height, std::string
textureID, int numFrames, int callbackID = 0, int animSpeed = 0) :
m_x(x),
m_y(y),
m_width(width),
m_height(height),
m_textureID(textureID),
m_numFrames(numFrames),
m_callbackID(callbackID),
m_animSpeed(animSpeed)
{

}
```

In other words, if the parameter is not passed in, then the default values will be used (0 in both cases). Rather than passing in a function pointer as `MenuButton` did, we are using `callbackID` to decide which callback function to use within a state. We can now start using our factory and parsing our states from an XML file.

Parsing states from an XML file

The file we will be parsing is the following (`test.xml` in source code downloads):

```
<?xml version="1.0" ?>
<STATES>
<MENU>
<TEXTURES>
  <texture filename="assets/button.png" ID="playbutton"/>
  <texture filename="assets/exit.png" ID="exitbutton"/>
</TEXTURES>

<OBJECTS>
  <object type="MenuButton" x="100" y="100" width="400"
  height="100" textureID="playbutton" numFrames="0"
  callbackID="1"/>
  <object type="MenuButton" x="100" y="300" width="400"
  height="100" textureID="exitbutton" numFrames="0"
  callbackID="2"/>
</OBJECTS>
</MENU>
```

```
<PLAY>
</PLAY>

<GAMEOVER>
</GAMEOVER>
</STATES>
```

We are going to create a new class that parses our states for us called `StateParser`. The `StateParser` class has no data members, it is to be used once in the `onEnter` function of a state and then discarded when it goes out of scope. Create a `StateParser.h` file and add the following code:

```
#include <iostream>
#include <vector>
#include "tinyxml.h"

class GameObject;

class StateParser
{
  public:

  bool parseState(const char* stateFile, std::string stateID,
  std::vector<GameObject*> *pObjects);

  private:

  void parseObjects(TiXmlElement* pStateRoot,
  std::vector<GameObject*> *pObjects);
  void parseTextures(TiXmlElement* pStateRoot,
  std::vector<std::string> *pTextureIDs);

};
```

We have three functions here, one public and two private. The `parseState` function takes the filename of an XML file as a parameter, along with the current `stateID` value and a pointer to `std::vector` of `GameObject*` for that state. The `StateParser.cpp` file will define this function:

```
bool StateParser::parseState(const char *stateFile, string
stateID, vector<GameObject *> *pObjects, std::vector<std::string>
*pTextureIDs)
{
  // create the XML document
  TiXmlDocument xmlDoc;

  // load the state file
```

Data-driven Design

```cpp
if(!xmlDoc.LoadFile(stateFile))
{
  cerr << xmlDoc.ErrorDesc() << "\n";
  return false;
}

// get the root element
TiXmlElement* pRoot = xmlDoc.RootElement();

// pre declare the states root node
TiXmlElement* pStateRoot = 0;
// get this states root node and assign it to pStateRoot
for(TiXmlElement* e = pRoot->FirstChildElement(); e != NULL; e = e->NextSiblingElement())
{
  if(e->Value() == stateID)
  {
    pStateRoot = e;
  }
}

// pre declare the texture root
TiXmlElement* pTextureRoot = 0;

// get the root of the texture elements
for(TiXmlElement* e = pStateRoot->FirstChildElement(); e != NULL; e = e->NextSiblingElement())
{
  if(e->Value() == string("TEXTURES"))
  {
    pTextureRoot = e;
  }
}

// now parse the textures
parseTextures(pTextureRoot, pTextureIDs);

// pre declare the object root node
TiXmlElement* pObjectRoot = 0;

// get the root node and assign it to pObjectRoot
for(TiXmlElement* e = pStateRoot->FirstChildElement(); e != NULL; e = e->NextSiblingElement())
{
```

```
      if(e->Value() == string("OBJECTS"))
      {
        pObjectRoot = e;
      }
    }

    // now parse the objects
    parseObjects(pObjectRoot, pObjects);

    return true;
  }
```

There is a lot of code in this function so it is worth covering in some depth. We will note the corresponding part of the XML file, along with the code we use, to obtain it. The first part of the function attempts to load the XML file that is passed into the function:

```
// create the XML document
TiXmlDocument xmlDoc;

// load the state file
if(!xmlDoc.LoadFile(stateFile))
{
  cerr << xmlDoc.ErrorDesc() << "\n";
  return false;
}
```

It displays an error to let you know what happened if the XML loading fails. Next we must grab the root node of the XML file:

```
// get the root element
TiXmlElement* pRoot = xmlDoc.RootElement(); // <STATES>
```

The rest of the nodes in the file are all children of this root node. We must now get the root node of the state we are currently parsing; let's say we are looking for MENU:

```
// declare the states root node
TiXmlElement* pStateRoot = 0;
// get this states root node and assign it to pStateRoot
for(TiXmlElement* e = pRoot->FirstChildElement(); e != NULL; e = e->NextSiblingElement())
{
  if(e->Value() == stateID)
  {
```

[143]

```
            pStateRoot = e;
        }
    }
```

This piece of code goes through each direct child of the root node and checks if its name is the same as `stateID`. Once it finds the correct node it assigns it to `pStateRoot`. We now have the root node of the state we want to parse.

```
<MENU> // the states root node
```

Now that we have a pointer to the root node of our state we can start to grab values from it. First we want to load the textures from the file so we look for the `<TEXTURE>` node using the children of the `pStateRoot` object we found before:

```
// pre declare the texture root
TiXmlElement* pTextureRoot = 0;

// get the root of the texture elements
for(TiXmlElement* e = pStateRoot->FirstChildElement(); e != NULL;
e = e->NextSiblingElement())
{
  if(e->Value() == string("TEXTURES"))
  {
    pTextureRoot = e;
  }
}
```

Once the `<TEXTURE>` node is found, we can pass it into the private `parseTextures` function (which we will cover a little later).

```
parseTextures(pTextureRoot, std::vector<std::string>
*pTextureIDs);
```

The function then moves onto searching for the `<OBJECT>` node and, once found, it passes it into the private `parseObjects` function. We also pass in the `pObjects` parameter:

```
    // pre declare the object root node
    TiXmlElement* pObjectRoot = 0;

    // get the root node and assign it to pObjectRoot
    for(TiXmlElement* e = pStateRoot->FirstChildElement(); e !=
    NULL; e = e->NextSiblingElement())
    {
      if(e->Value() == string("OBJECTS"))
      {
        pObjectRoot = e;
```

```
    }
  }
  parseObjects(pObjectRoot, pObjects);
  return true;
}
```

At this point our state has been parsed. We can now cover the two private functions, starting with `parseTextures`.

```
void StateParser::parseTextures(TiXmlElement* pStateRoot,
std::vector<std::string> *pTextureIDs)
{
  for(TiXmlElement* e = pStateRoot->FirstChildElement(); e !=
  NULL; e = e->NextSiblingElement())
  {
    string filenameAttribute = e->Attribute("filename");
    string idAttribute = e->Attribute("ID");
    pTextureIDs->push_back(idAttribute); // push into list

    TheTextureManager::Instance()->load(filenameAttribute,
    idAttribute, TheGame::Instance()->getRenderer());
  }
}
```

This function gets the `filename` and `ID` attributes from each of the texture values in this part of the XML:

```
<TEXTURES>
  <texture filename="button.png" ID="playbutton"/>
  <texture filename="exit.png" ID="exitbutton"/>
</TEXTURES>
```

It then adds them to `TextureManager`.

```
TheTextureManager::Instance()->load(filenameAttribute,
idAttribute, TheGame::Instance()->getRenderer());
```

The `parseObjects` function is quite a bit more complicated. It creates objects using our `GameObjectFactory` function and reads from this part of the XML file:

```
<OBJECTS>
  <object type="MenuButton" x="100" y="100" width="400"
  height="100" textureID="playbutton" numFrames="0"
  callbackID="1"/>
  <object type="MenuButton" x="100" y="300" width="400"
  height="100" textureID="exitbutton" numFrames="0"
  callbackID="2"/>
</OBJECTS>
```

Data-driven Design

The `parseObjects` function is defined like so:

```cpp
void StateParser::parseObjects(TiXmlElement *pStateRoot,
std::vector<GameObject *> *pObjects)
{
  for(TiXmlElement* e = pStateRoot->FirstChildElement(); e !=
  NULL; e = e->NextSiblingElement())
  {
    int x, y, width, height, numFrames, callbackID, animSpeed;
    string textureID;

    e->Attribute("x", &x);
    e->Attribute("y", &y);
    e->Attribute("width",&width);
    e->Attribute("height", &height);
    e->Attribute("numFrames", &numFrames);
    e->Attribute("callbackID", &callbackID);
    e->Attribute("animSpeed", &animSpeed);

    textureID = e->Attribute("textureID");

    GameObject* pGameObject = TheGameObjectFactory::Instance()
    ->create(e->Attribute("type"));
    pGameObject->load(new LoaderParams
    (x,y,width,height,textureID,numFrames,callbackID, animSpeed));
    pObjects->push_back(pGameObject);
  }
}
```

First we get any values we need from the current node. Since XML files are pure text, we cannot simply grab ints or floats from the file. TinyXML has functions with which you can pass in the value you want to be set and the attribute name. For example:

```cpp
e->Attribute("x", &x);
```

This sets the variable x to the value contained within attribute `"x"`. Next comes the creation of a `GameObject*` class using the factory.

```cpp
GameObject* pGameObject = TheGameObjectFactory::Instance()-
>create(e->Attribute("type"));
```

We pass in the value from the `type` attribute and use that to create the correct object from the factory. After this we must use the `load` function of `GameObject` to set our desired values using the values loaded from the XML file.

```cpp
pGameObject->load(new
LoaderParams(x,y,width,height,textureID,numFrames,callbackID));
```

And finally we push `pGameObject` into the `pObjects` array, which is actually a pointer to the current state's object vector.

```
pObjects->push_back(pGameObject);
```

Loading the menu state from an XML file

We now have most of our state loading code in place and can make use of this in the `MenuState` class. First we must do a little legwork and set up a new way of assigning the callbacks to our `MenuButton` objects, since this is not something we could pass in from an XML file. The approach we will take is to give any object that wants to make use of a callback an attribute named `callbackID` in the XML file. Other objects do not need this value and `LoaderParams` will use the default value of 0. The `MenuButton` class will make use of this value and pull it from its `LoaderParams`, like so:

```
void MenuButton::load(const LoaderParams *pParams)
{
  SDLGameObject::load(pParams);
  m_callbackID = pParams->getCallbackID();
  m_currentFrame = MOUSE_OUT;
}
```

The `MenuButton` class will also need two other functions, one to set the callback function and another to return its callback ID:

```
void setCallback(void(*callback)()) { m_callback = callback;}
int getCallbackID() { return m_callbackID; }
```

Next we must create a function to set callbacks. Any state that uses objects with callbacks will need an implementation of this function. The most likely states to have callbacks are menu states, so we will rename our `MenuState` class to `MainMenuState` and make `MenuState` an abstract class that extends from `GameState`. The class will declare a function that sets the callbacks for any items that need it and it will also have a vector of the `Callback` objects as a member; this will be used within the `setCallbacks` function for each state.

```
class MenuState : public GameState
{
  protected:

  typedef void(*Callback)();
  virtual void setCallbacks(const std::vector<Callback>& callbacks)
  = 0;

  std::vector<Callback> m_callbacks;
};
```

Data-driven Design

The `MainMenuState` class (previously `MenuState`) will now derive from this `MenuState` class.

```cpp
#include "MenuState.h"
#include "GameObject.h"

class MainMenuState : public MenuState
{
  public:

  virtual void update();
  virtual void render();

  virtual bool onEnter();
  virtual bool onExit();

  virtual std::string getStateID() const { return s_menuID; }

  private:

  virtual void setCallbacks(const std::vector<Callback>&
  callbacks);

  // call back functions for menu items
  static void s_menuToPlay();
  static void s_exitFromMenu();

  static const std::string s_menuID;

  std::vector<GameObject*> m_gameObjects;
};
```

Because `MainMenuState` now derives from `MenuState`, it must of course declare and define the `setCallbacks` function. We are now ready to use our state parsing to load the `MainMenuState` class. Our `onEnter` function will now look like this:

```cpp
bool MainMenuState::onEnter()
{
  // parse the state
  StateParser stateParser;
  stateParser.parseState("test.xml", s_menuID, &m_gameObjects,
  &m_textureIDList);
```

```
    m_callbacks.push_back(0); //pushback 0 callbackID start from 1
    m_callbacks.push_back(s_menuToPlay);
    m_callbacks.push_back(s_exitFromMenu);

    // set the callbacks for menu items
    setCallbacks(m_callbacks);

    std::cout << "entering MenuState\n";
    return true;
}
```

We create a state parser and then use it to parse the current state. We push any callbacks into the m_callbacks array inherited from MenuState. Now we need to define the setCallbacks function:

```
void MainMenuState::setCallbacks(const std::vector<Callback>&
callbacks)
{
  // go through the game objects
  for(int i = 0; i < m_gameObjects.size(); i++)
  {
    // if they are of type MenuButton then assign a callback
    // based on the id passed in from the file
    if(dynamic_cast<MenuButton*>(m_gameObjects[i]))
    {
      MenuButton* pButton =
      dynamic_cast<MenuButton*>(m_gameObjects[i]);
      pButton->setCallback(callbacks[pButton->getCallbackID()]);
    }
  }
}
```

We use dynamic_cast to check whether the object is a MenuButton type; if it is then we do the actual cast and then use the objects callbackID as the index into the callbacks vector and assign the correct function. While this method of assigning callbacks could be seen as not very extendable and could possibly be better implemented, it does have a redeeming feature; it allows us to keep our callbacks inside the state they will need to be called from. This means that we won't need a huge header file with all of the callbacks in.

Data-driven Design

One last alteration we need is to add a list of texture IDs to each state so that we can clear all of the textures that were loaded for that state. Open up `GameState.h` and we will add a `protected` variable.

```
protected:
std::vector<std::string> m_textureIDList;
```

We will pass this into the state parser in `onEnter` and then we can clear any used textures in the `onExit` function of each state, like so:

```
// clear the texture manager
for(int i = 0; i < m_textureIDList.size(); i++)
{
  TheTextureManager::Instance()->
  clearFromTextureMap(m_textureIDList[i]);
}
```

Before we start running the game we need to register our `MenuButton` type with the `GameObjectFactory`. Open up `Game.cpp` and in the `Game::init` function we can register the type.

```
TheGameObjectFactory::Instance()->registerType("MenuButton", new MenuButtonCreator());
```

We can now run the game and see our fully data-driven `MainMenuState`.

Loading other states from an XML file

Our `MainMenuState` class now loads from an XML file. We need to make our other states do the same. We will only cover the code that has changed, so assume that everything else has remained the same when following through this section.

Loading the play state

We will start with `PlayState.cpp` and its `onEnter` function.

```
bool PlayState::onEnter()
{
  // parse the state
  StateParser stateParser;
  stateParser.parseState("test.xml", s_playID, &m_gameObjects,
  &m_textureIDList);

  std::cout << "entering PlayState\n";
  return true;
}
```

[150]

We must also add the new texture clearing code that we had in `MainMenuState` to the `onExit` function.

```
// clear the texture manager
for(int i = 0; i < m_textureIDList.size(); i++)
{
  TheTextureManager::Instance()->
  clearFromTextureMap(m_textureIDList[i]);
}
```

These are the only alterations that we will need to do here but we must also update our XML file to have something to load in `PlayState`.

```
<PLAY>
<TEXTURES>
  <texture filename="helicopter.png" ID="helicopter"/>
  <texture filename="helicopter2.png" ID="helicopter2"/>
</TEXTURES>

<OBJECTS>
  <object type="Player" x="500" y="100" width="128" height="55"
  textureID="helicopter" numFrames="4"/>
  <object type="Enemy" x="100" y="100" width="128" height="55"
  textureID="helicopter2" numFrames="4"/>
</OBJECTS>
</PLAY>
```

Our `Enemy` object will now need to set its initial velocity in its load function rather than the constructor, otherwise the `load` function would override it.

```
void Enemy::load(const LoaderParams *pParams)
{
  SDLGameObject::load(pParams);
  m_velocity.setY(2);
}
```

Finally we must register these objects with the factory. We can do this in the `Game::init` function just like the `MenuButton` object.

```
TheGameObjectFactory::Instance()->registerType("Player", new
PlayerCreator());
TheGameObjectFactory::Instance()->registerType("Enemy", new
EnemyCreator());
```

Loading the pause state

Our `PauseState` class must now inherit from `MenuState` as we want it to contain callbacks. We must update the `PauseState.h` file to first inherit from `MenuState`.

```
class PauseState : public MenuState
```

We must also declare the `setCallbacks` function.

```
virtual void setCallbacks(const std::vector<Callback>& callbacks);
```

Now we must update the `PauseState.cpp` file, starting with the `onEnter` function.

```
bool PauseState::onEnter()
{
  StateParser stateParser;
  stateParser.parseState("test.xml", s_pauseID, &m_gameObjects,
  &m_textureIDList);

  m_callbacks.push_back(0);
  m_callbacks.push_back(s_pauseToMain);
  m_callbacks.push_back(s_resumePlay);

  setCallbacks(m_callbacks);

  std::cout << "entering PauseState\n";
  return true;
}
```

The `setCallbacks` function is exactly like `MainMenuState`.

```
void PauseState::setCallbacks(const std::vector<Callback>&
callbacks)
{
  // go through the game objects
  for(int i = 0; i < m_gameObjects.size(); i++)
  {
    // if they are of type MenuButton then assign a callback based
    on the id passed in from the file
    if(dynamic_cast<MenuButton*>(m_gameObjects[i]))
    {
      MenuButton* pButton =
      dynamic_cast<MenuButton*>(m_gameObjects[i]);
      pButton->setCallback(callbacks[pButton->getCallbackID()]);
    }
  }
}
```

Finally we must add the texture clearing code to `onExit`.

```
// clear the texture manager
for(int i = 0; i < m_textureIDList.size(); i++)
{
  TheTextureManager::Instance()->
  clearFromTextureMap(m_textureIDList[i]);
}
```

And then update our XML file to include this state.

```
<PAUSE>
<TEXTURES>
  <texture filename="resume.png" ID="resumebutton"/>
  <texture filename="main.png" ID="mainbutton"/>
</TEXTURES>

<OBJECTS>
  <object type="MenuButton" x="200" y="100" width="200"
  height="80" textureID="mainbutton" numFrames="0"
  callbackID="1"/>
  <object type="MenuButton" x="200" y="300" width="200"
  height="80" textureID="resumebutton" numFrames="0"
  callbackID="2"/>
</OBJECTS>
</PAUSE>
```

Loading the game over state

Our final state is `GameOverState`. Again this will be very similar to other states and we will only cover what has changed. Since we want `GameOverState` to handle callbacks it will now inherit from `MenuState`.

```
class GameOverState : public MenuState
```

We will then declare the `setCallbacks` function.

```
virtual void setCallbacks(const std::vector<Callback>& callbacks);
```

The `onEnter` function should be looking very familiar now.

```
bool GameOverState::onEnter()
{
  // parse the state
  StateParser stateParser;
  stateParser.parseState("test.xml", s_gameOverID, &m_gameObjects,
  &m_textureIDList);
```

Data-driven Design

```cpp
    m_callbacks.push_back(0);
    m_callbacks.push_back(s_gameOverToMain);
    m_callbacks.push_back(s_restartPlay);

    // set the callbacks for menu items
    setCallbacks(m_callbacks);

    std::cout << "entering PauseState\n";
    return true;
}
```

The texture clearing method is the same as in the previous states, so we will leave you to implement that yourself. In fact `onExit` is looking so similar between states that it would be a good idea to make a generic implementation for it in `GameState` and just use that; again we will leave that to you.

You may have noticed the similarity between the `onEnter` functions. It would be great to have a default `onEnter` implementation but, unfortunately, due to the need to specify different callback functions, our callback implementation will not allow this and this is one of its main flaws.

Our `AnimatedGraphic` class will now need to grab the `animSpeed` value from `LoaderParams` in its `load` function.

```cpp
void AnimatedGraphic::load(const LoaderParams *pParams)
{
  SDLGameObject::load(pParams);
  m_animSpeed = pParams->getAnimSpeed();
}
```

We will also have to register this type with `GameObjectFactory`.

```cpp
TheGameObjectFactory::Instance()->registerType("AnimatedGraphic",
new AnimatedGraphicCreator());
```

And finally we can update the XML file to include this state:

```xml
<GAMEOVER>
<TEXTURES>
  <texture filename="gameover.png" ID="gameovertext"/>
  <texture filename="main.png" ID="mainbutton"/>
  <texture filename="restart.png" ID="restartbutton"/>
</TEXTURES>

<OBJECTS>
```

```
        <object type="AnimatedGraphic" x="200" y="100" width="190"
        height="30" textureID="gameovertext" numFrames="2"
        animSpeed="2"/>
        <object type="MenuButton" x="200" y="200" width="200"
        height="80" textureID="mainbutton" numFrames="0"
        callbackID="1"/>
        <object type="MenuButton" x="200" y="300" width="200"
        height="80" textureID="restartbutton" numFrames="0"
        callbackID="2"/>
    </OBJECTS>
</GAMEOVER>
```

We now have all of our states loading from the XML file and one of the biggest benefits of this is that you do not have to recompile the game when you change a value. Go ahead and change the XML file to move positions or even use different textures for objects; if the XML is saved then you can just run the game again and it will use the new values. This is a huge time saver for us and gives us complete control over a state without the need to recompile our game.

Summary

Loading data from external files is an extremely useful tool in programming games. This chapter enabled our game to do this and applied it to all of our existing states. We also covered how the use of factories enabled us to create objects dynamically at runtime. The next chapter will cover even more data-driven design as well as tile maps so that we can really decouple our game and allow it to use external sources rather than hardcoded values.

7
Creating and Displaying Tile Maps

Most 2D games that you have played in the past made use of **tile maps**. It is an extremely efficient and fast way to develop complex 2D levels or scenes. Even if a game has more complex graphical content, it is likely that it will still make use of tiles in some way. Throughout this chapter we will be using the **tiled map editor**, an open source and cross-platform tool created by Thorbjørn Lindeijer and a large open source community. It is available at http://www.mapeditor.org/. We will essentially make this tool our level editor and use it for creating maps and placing our objects within those maps.

In this chapter we will cover:

- What a tile map is
- What a tile sheet looks like
- Using the tiled map editor to create our maps
- Parsing a state from a tiled map
- Loading and displaying a tile-based map in SDL 2.0

Creating and Displaying Tile Maps

What is a tile map?

If you have played a lot of 2D games then you will be very familiar with tile maps. We will start by looking at an example in the form of the following screenshot:

This 20 x 15 tile map was made using the following screenshot called a **tileset**.

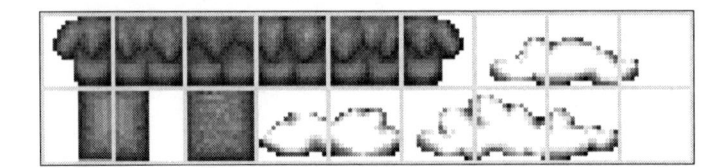

Chapter 7

As you can see, one huge advantage to a tile system like this is that you can create large maps from relatively small image files. Tile maps are essentially a multidimensional array of IDs that tell us which part of the tileset we want to draw at each location. It will help to look at the images again with their IDs in place as shown in the following screenshot:

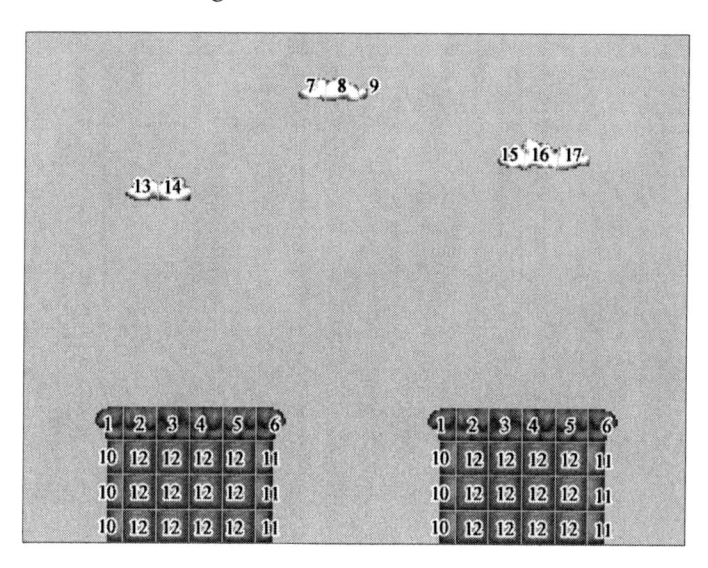

Here is the tileset with its IDs in place as shown in the preceding screenshot.

To draw the map we loop through the number of columns and the number of rows, grab the correct tile using its ID, and draw it to the screen. Any tile with an ID of zero will not be drawn (a blank tile). This can be seen in the preceding screenshot.

Getting familiar with the Tiled application

Tiled is a very user-friendly application that can greatly speed up our development time. Once you have downloaded and installed the application, open it up and you will be presented with the user interface as shown in the following screenshot:

On the right-hand side we have the **Layers** and **Tilesets** views; the left-hand side will contain our tile map. First we must create a new map, this can be done by navigating to **File** | **New...** or *Ctrl + N*. This brings up the new map dialog as shown in the following screenshot:

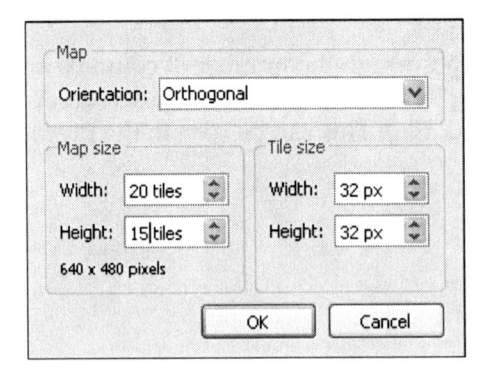

Here we can define the size and type of our map. We are only going to use orthogonal tile maps (as opposed to isometric), so go ahead and create an orthogonal tile map that is 20 tiles wide and 15 tiles high, with tile width and height both set to 32 px. We can now see our tile map in the left-hand side of the UI (*Ctrl* + *G* will show the grid). Tiled will also automatically create a layer for us called **Tile Layer 1** (Visible in the **Layers** view on the right-hand side) as shown in the following screenshot:

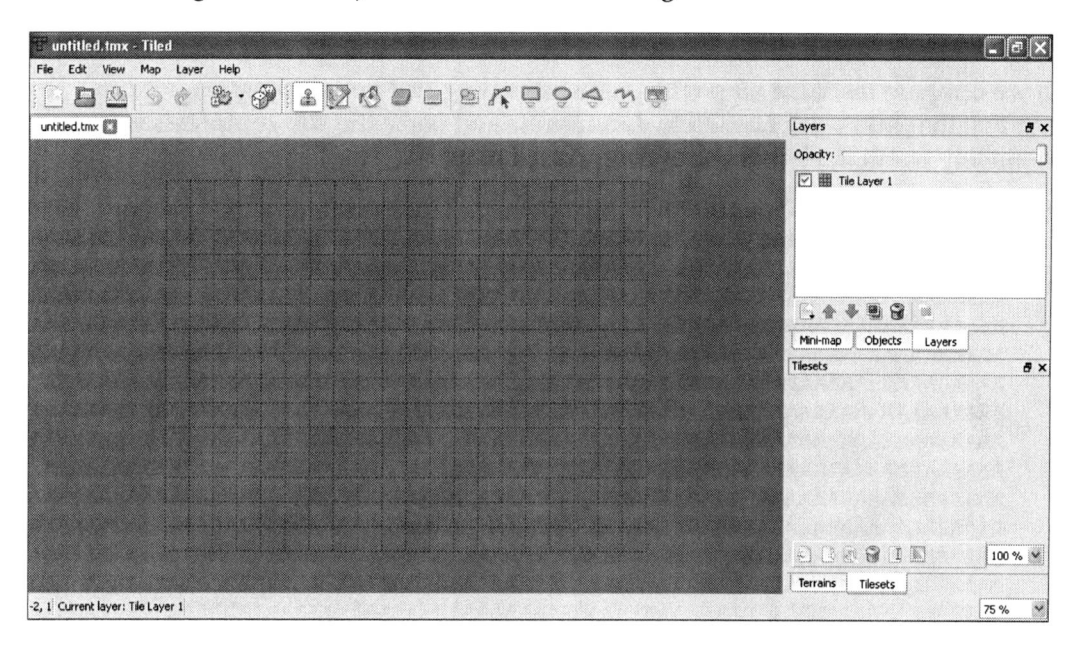

We are not going to deal with any terrain so we can turn off that tab by navigating to **View** | **Terrains** and unchecking. Save this map as `map1.tmx` in the same location as the rest of our game assets. If you open this file you will see that it is actually just an XML file:

```
<?xml version="1.0" encoding="UTF-8"?>
<map version="1.0" orientation="orthogonal" width="20" height="15"
  tilewidth="32" tileheight="32">
    <layer name="Tile Layer 1" width="20" height="15">
        <data encoding="base64" compression="zlib">
          eJxjYBgFo2AUjIKhAQAEsAAB
        </data>
    </layer>
</map>
```

Creating and Displaying Tile Maps

This should all look very familiar. Tiled has a few different compression algorithms that can be used to store the tile IDs of our maps. The preceding file uses the **zlib compression algorithm** along with **base64 encoding** which, as you can see, gives great results:

```
<data encoding="base64" compression="zlib">
  eJxjYBgFo2AUjIKhAQAEsAAB
</data>
```

If we compare the same map with base64 encoding and no compression, we can see that the extra work needed to decompress and parse the zlib compression is definitely worth it. Here is the uncompressed map:

```
<data encoding="base64">
AAAAAAAAAAAAAAAAAAAAAAAAAAAAAAAAAAAAAAAAAAAAAAAAAAAAAAAAAAAAAAAA
AAAAAAAAAAAAAAAAAAAAAAAAAAAAAAAAAAAAAAAAAAAAAAAAAAAAAAAAAAAAAAAA
AAAAAAAAAAAAAAAAAAAAAAAAAAAAAAAAAAAAAAAAAAAAAAAAAAAAAAAAAAAAAAAA
AAAAAAAAAAAAAAAAAAAAAAAAAAAAAAAAAAAAAAAAAAAAAAAAAAAAAAAAAAAAAAAA
AAAAAAAAAAAAAAAAAAAAAAAAAAAAAAAAAAAAAAAAAAAAAAAAAAAAAAAAAAAAAAAA
AAAAAAAAAAAAAAAAAAAAAAAAAAAAAAAAAAAAAAAAAAAAAAAAAAAAAAAAAAAAAA
AAAAAAAAAAAAAAAAAAAAAAAAAAAAAAAAAAAAAAAAAAAAAAAAAAAAAAAAAAAAAAAA
AAAAAAAAAAAAAAAAAAAAAAAAAAAAAAAAAAAAAAAAAAAAAAAAAAAAAAAAAAAAAAAA
AAAAAAAAAAAAAAAAAAAAAAAAAAAAAAAAAAAAAAAAAAAAAAAAAAAAAAAAAAAAAA
AAAAAAAAAAAAAAAAAAAAAAAAAAAAAAAAAAAAAAAAAAAAAAAAAAAAAAAAAAAAAAAA
AAAAAAAAAAAAAAAAAAAAAAAAAAAAAAAAAAAAAAAAAAAAAAAAAAAAAAAAAAAAAAAA
AAAAAAAAAAAAAAAAAAAAAAAAAAAAAAAAAAAAAAAAAAAAAAAAAAAAAAAAAAAAAAAA
AAAAAAAAAAAAAAAAAAAAAAAAAAAAAAAAAAAAAAAAAAAAAAAAAAAAAAAAAAAAAAAA
AAAAAAAAAAAAAAAAAAAAAAAAAAAAAAAAAAAAAAAAAAAAAAAAAAAAAAAAAAAAAAAA
AAAAAAAAAAAAAAAAAAAAAAAAAAAAAAAAAAAAAAAAAAAAAAAAAAAAAAAAAAAAAAAA
AAAAAAAAAAAAAAAAAAAAAAAAAAAAAAAAAAAAAAAAAAAAAAAAAAAAAAAAAAAAAAAA
AAAAAAAAAAAAAAAAAAAAAAAAAAAAAAAAAAAAAAAAAAAAAAAAAAAAAAAAAAAAAAAA
AAAAAAAAAAAAAAAAAAAAAAAAAAAAAAAAAAAAAAAAAAAAAAAAAAAAAAAAAAAAAAAA
AAAAAAAAAAAAAAAAAAAAAAAAAAAAAAAAAAAAAAAAAAAAAAAAAAAAAAAAAAAAAAAA
AAAAAAAAAAAAAAAAAAAAAAAAAAAAAAAAAAAAAAAAAAAAAAAAAAAAAAAAAAAAAA
</data>
```

We will cover this in more depth once we start parsing the tile maps, but for now let's look at adding a tileset. Navigate to **Map | New Tileset...** and it will bring up a new **Tileset** dialog as shown in the following screenshot:

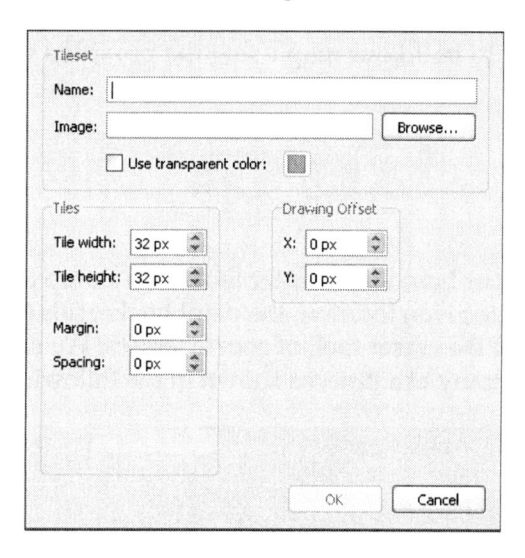

The tileset we will start with is `blocks1.png` as shown in the following screenshot, available in the source downloads.

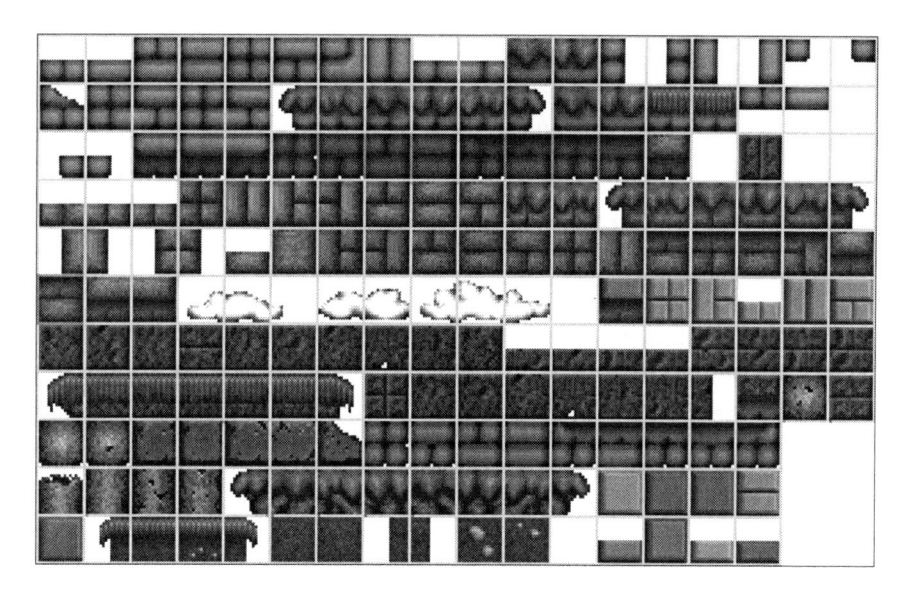

Copy the image to the game assets location and then we can browse to it in the **New Tileset** dialog. This tileset has a 2 pixel wide margin around the outside and 2 pixel spacing between each tile; each tile is 32 x 32 pixels. Once these values are set, click on **OK** and the tileset will appear in the **Tilesets** view to the right-hand side. We can now start to build our map using the provided tools as shown in the following screenshot:

The red highlights are our bread-and-butter tools. The stamp tool adds the selected tile from the tileset to the given location, the paint bucket fills an area with a selected tile from the tileset, and the eraser tool, of course, erases. We can select tiles from the tileset one at a time or many at a time, as shown in the following screenshot:

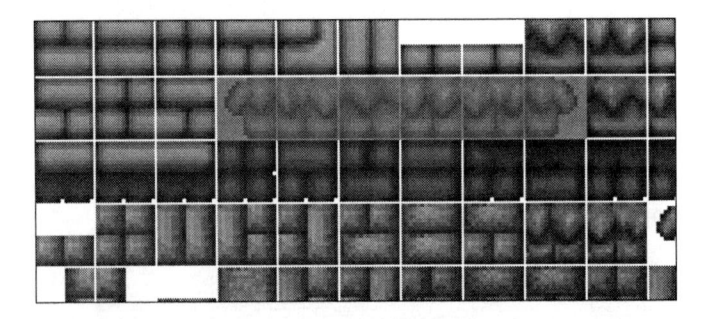

Go ahead and get acquainted with these tools by building a simple map. Once the map is saved we will see that the tileset has been added to the map file:

```
<tileset firstgid="1" name="blocks1" tilewidth="32" tileheight="32"
  spacing="2" margin="2">
  <image source="assets/blocks1.png" width="614" height="376"/>
</tileset>
```

The `firstgid` attribute is the first tile ID that uses this tileset. If we were to have more than one tileset, it would come with its own `firstgid` attribute so that we knew which tile IDs to start associating with that tileset; again, we will cover this in greater detail when we come to parse our maps. Add another tileset, `blocks2.png` (also available in the source code downloads), to our map and we shall move into drawing it in our game.

Parsing and drawing a tile map

Now that we are relatively familiar with creating tile maps in the Tiled application we will move on to parsing them and drawing them in our game. We are going to create quite a few new classes starting with a class called `Level` that will hold our tilesets and also draw and update our separate layers. Let's go ahead and create `Level.h` in our project and add the following code:

```
class Level
{
  public:

  Level();
  ~Level() {}

  void update();
  void render();
};
```

We will also define a `struct` at the top of this file called `Tileset`:

```
struct Tileset
{
  int firstGridID;
  int tileWidth;
  int tileHeight;
  int spacing;
  int margin;
  int width;
  int height;
  int numColumns;
  std::string name;
};
```

This `struct` holds any information we need to know about our tilesets. Our `Level` class will now also hold a vector of `Tileset` objects:

```
private:

  std::vector<Tileset> m_tilesets;
```

Next we will create a public getter function that returns a pointer to this `Tileset` vector:

```
std::vector<Tileset>* getTilesets()
{
    return &m_tilesets;
}
```

We will pass this into our parser when we come to load the map.

The next class we will create is an abstract base class called `Layer`. All of our layer types will derive from this class. Create `Layer.h` and add the following code:

```
class Layer
{
  public:

    virtual void render() = 0;
    virtual void update() = 0;

  protected:

    virtual ~Layer() {}
};
```

Now that we have the `Layer` class we will store a vector of the `Layer*` objects in the `Level` class. Back in `Level.h` add our vector:

```
std::vector<Layer*> m_layers;
```

And a getter function:

```
std::vector<Layer*>* getLayers()
{
    return &m_layers;
}
```

Now we have a basic `Level` class in place; its purpose is to store, draw, and update our layers. We will define the functions for `Level` in a `Level.cpp` file:

```
void Level::render()
{
  for(int i = 0; i < m _layers.size(); i++)
  {
    m_layers[i]->render();
  }
}
void Level::update()
{
  for(int i = 0; i < m_layers.size(); i++)
  {
    m_layers[i]->update();
  }
}
```

Creating the TileLayer class

Our first layer type is going to be a `TileLayer`. This type of layer is made up entirely of tiles and does not contain anything else. We have already created a layer like this in the Tiled application. Create `TileLayer.h` and we can start to write up this class:

```
class TileLayer : public Layer
{
  public:

    TileLayer(int tileSize, const std::vector<Tileset> &tilesets);

    virtual void update();
    virtual void render();

    void setTileIDs(const std::vector<std::vector<int>>& data)
    {
        m_tileIDs = data;
    }

    void setTileSize(int tileSize)
    {
        m_tileSize = tileSize;
    }

    Tileset getTilesetByID(int tileID);

  private:

    int m_numColumns;
    int m_numRows;
    int m_tileSize;

    Vector2D m_position;
    Vector2D m_velocity;

    const std::vector<Tileset> &m_tilesets;

    std::vector<std::vector<int>> m_tileIDs;
};
```

There is nothing too complicated about this class; it holds data for our tile layer. The `Vector2D` variables are used when we start to scroll our maps. We will not define this class' functions properly right now, but you will need to create empty definitions along with defining the vector constants in a `TileLayer.cpp` file.

Creating and Displaying Tile Maps

Creating the LevelParser class

Now that we have the basic level and layer classes in place, we can move onto creating a parser for our `.tmx` files and creating levels from them. Create `LevelParser.h`:

```
Class LevelParser
{
  public:

    Level* parseLevel(const char* levelFile);

  private:

    void parseTilesets(TiXmlElement* pTilesetRoot,
      std::vector<Tileset>* pTilesets);

    void parseTileLayer(TiXmlElement* pTileElement,
      std::vector<Layer*> *pLayers, const std::vector<Tileset>*
        pTilesets);

    int m_tileSize;
    int m_width;
    int m_height;
};
```

The `parseLevel` function is what we will call whenever we want to create a level. To ensure that this function must be used to create a `Level` object, we will make the `Level` class' constructor private and make it a friend class of `LevelParser`:

```
private:

  friend class LevelParser;
  Level();
```

Now `LevelParser` has access to the private constructor of `Level` and can return new instances. We can now define the `parseLevel` function and then go through it step-by-step. Create `LevelParser.cpp` and define the `parseLevel` function as follows:

```
Level* LevelParser::parseLevel(const char *levelFile)
{
    // create a TinyXML document and load the map XML
    TiXmlDocument levelDocument;
    levelDocument.LoadFile(levelFile);

    // create the level object
```

[168]

```
        Level* pLevel = new Level();

        // get the root node
        TiXmlElement* pRoot = levelDocument.RootElement();

        pRoot->Attribute("tilewidth", &m_tileSize);
        pRoot->Attribute("width", &m_width);
        pRoot->Attribute("height", &m_height);

        // parse the tilesets
        for(TiXmlElement* e = pRoot->FirstChildElement(); e != NULL; e =
          e->NextSiblingElement())
        {
          if(e->Value() == std::string("tileset"))
          {
             parseTilesets(e, pLevel->getTilesets());
          }
        }

        // parse any object layers
        for(TiXmlElement* e = pRoot->FirstChildElement(); e != NULL; e =
          e->NextSiblingElement())
        {
          if(e->Value() == std::string("layer"))
          {
            parseTileLayer(e, pLevel->getLayers(), pLevel->getTilesets());
          }
        }

        return pLevel;
}
```

We covered XML files and TinyXML in the previous chapter so I won't go into detail again here. The first part of the function grabs the root node:

```
    // get the root node
    TiXmlElement* pRoot = levelDocument.RootElement();
```

We can see from the map file that this node has several attributes:

```
    <map version="1.0" orientation="orthogonal" width="60" height="15"
      tilewidth="32" tileheight="32">
```

Creating and Displaying Tile Maps

We grab these values using the `Attribute` function from TinyXML and set the member variables of `LevelParser`:

```
pRoot->Attribute("tilewidth", &m_tileSize);
pRoot->Attribute("width", &m_width);
pRoot->Attribute("height", &m_height);
```

Next we must check for any tileset nodes and parse them, using the `getTilesets` function of our newly created `Level` instance to pass in the `Tileset` vector:

```
// parse the tilesets
for(TiXmlElement* e = pRoot->FirstChildElement(); e != NULL; e =
  e->NextSiblingElement())
{
  if(e->Value() == std::string("tileset"))
  {
    parseTilesets(e, pLevel->getTilesets());
  }
}
```

Finally we can check for any tile layers and then parse them, again using the getter functions from our `pLevel` object, which we then return:

```
// parse any object layers
for(TiXmlElement* e = pRoot->FirstChildElement(); e != NULL; e =
  e->NextSiblingElement())
{
  if(e->Value() == std::string("layer"))
  {
    parseTileLayer(e, pLevel->getLayers(), pLevel->getTilesets());
  }
}

return pLevel;
}
```

You can see that this function is very similar to our `parseState` function from the previous chapter. Now we must define the `parseTilesets` and `parseTileLayer` functions.

Parsing tilesets

Parsing tilesets is actually quite simple due to our `TextureManager` class:

```
void LevelParser::parseTilesets(TiXmlElement* pTilesetRoot,
  std::vector<Tileset>* pTilesets)
{
```

```cpp
// first add the tileset to texture manager
    TheTextureManager::Instance()->load(pTilesetRoot-
>FirstChildElement()->Attribute("source"), pTilesetRoot-
>Attribute("name"), TheGame::Instance()->getRenderer());

// create a tileset object
Tileset tileset;
pTilesetRoot->FirstChildElement()->Attribute("width",
    &tileset.width);
pTilesetRoot->FirstChildElement()->Attribute("height",
    &tileset.height);
pTilesetRoot->Attribute("firstgid", &tileset.firstGridID);
pTilesetRoot->Attribute("tilewidth", &tileset.tileWidth);
pTilesetRoot->Attribute("tileheight", &tileset.tileHeight);
pTilesetRoot->Attribute("spacing", &tileset.spacing);
pTilesetRoot->Attribute("margin", &tileset.margin);
tileset.name = pTilesetRoot->Attribute("name");

tileset.numColumns = tileset.width / (tileset.tileWidth +
    tileset.spacing);

pTilesets->push_back(tileset);
}
```

We add the tileset to the `TextureManager` class using its attributes and then create a `Tileset` object and push it into the `pTilesets` array. The `pTilesets` array is actually a pointer to the array from our `pLevel` object which we previously created in the `parseLevel` function. Here is our first tileset so that you can look at it alongside the preceding function:

```xml
<tileset firstgid="1" name="blocks1" tilewidth="32" tileheight="32"
    spacing="2" margin="2">
    <image source="blocks1.png" width="614" height="376"/>
</tileset>
```

Parsing a tile layer

Due to the compression and encoding of our tile IDs, this function is actually quite complicated. We are going to make use of a few different libraries that will help us to decode and decompress our data, the first of which is a **Base64** decoder. We will be using a decoder created by René Nyffenegger, available from the source code downloads and also from https://github.com/ReneNyffenegger/development_misc/tree/master/base64. The `base64.h` and `base64.cpp` files can be added directly to the project.

Creating and Displaying Tile Maps

The second library we will need is the `zlib` library, a compiled version is available at http://www.zlib.net and can be easily added to your project like any other library. Once these libraries are available to the project we can start parsing our tiles:

```
void LevelParser::parseTileLayer(TiXmlElement* pTileElement,
  std::vector<Layer*> *pLayers, const std::vector<Tileset>*
  pTilesets)
{
  TileLayer* pTileLayer = new TileLayer(m_tileSize, *pTilesets);

    // tile data
  std::vector<std::vector<int>> data;

  std::string decodedIDs;
  TiXmlElement* pDataNode;

  for(TiXmlElement* e = pTileElement->FirstChildElement(); e !=
    NULL; e = e->NextSiblingElement())
  {
    if(e->Value() == std::string("data"))
    {
      pDataNode = e;
    }
  }

  for(TiXmlNode* e = pDataNode->FirstChild(); e != NULL; e =
    e->NextSibling())
  {
    TiXmlText* text = e->ToText();
    std::string t = text->Value();
    decodedIDs = base64_decode(t);
  }

    // uncompress zlib compression
  uLongf numGids = m_width * m_height * sizeof(int);
  std::vector<unsigned> gids(numGids);
  uncompress((Bytef*)&gids[0], &numGids, (const
    Bytef*)decodedIDs.c_str(), decodedIDs.size());

  std::vector<int> layerRow(m_width);

  for(int j = 0; j < m_height; j++)
  {
    data.push_back(layerRow);
  }

  for(int rows = 0; rows < m_height; rows++)
```

```
    {
      for(int cols = 0; cols < m_width; cols++)
      {
        data[rows][cols] = gids[rows * m_width + cols];
      }
    }

    pTileLayer->setTileIDs(data);

    pLayers->push_back(pTileLayer);
}
```

Let's go through this function step-by-step. First we create a new TileLayer instance:

```
TileLayer* pTileLayer = new TileLayer(m_tileSize, *pTilesets);
```

Next we declare some needed variables; a multidimensional array of int values to hold our final decoded and uncompressed tile data, a std::string that will be our base64 decoded information and finally a place to store our XML node once we find it:

```
// tiledata
std::vector<std::vector<int>> data;

std::string decodedIDs;
TiXmlElement* pDataNode;
```

We can search for the node we need in the same way we have previously done:

```
for(TiXmlElement* e = pTileElement->FirstChildElement(); e !=
  NULL; e = e->NextSiblingElement())
{
   if(e->Value() == std::string("data"))
   {
     pDataNode = e;
   }
}
```

Once we have found the correct node we can then get the text from within it (our encoded/compressed data) and use the base64 decoder to decode it:

```
for(TiXmlNode* e = pDataNode->FirstChild(); e != NULL; e =
e->NextSibling())
{
  TiXmlText* text = e->ToText();
```

Creating and Displaying Tile Maps

```
    std::string t = text->Value();
    decodedIDs = base64_decode(t);
}
```

Our `decodedIDs` variable is now a `base64` decoded `string`. The next step is to use the `zlib` library to decompress our data, this is done using the `uncompress` function:

```
// uncompress zlib compression
uLongf sizeofids = m_width * m_height * sizeof(int);

std::vector<int> ids(m_width * m_height);

uncompress((Bytef*)&ids[0],
   &sizeofids,(const Bytef*)decodedIDs.c_str(), decodedIDs.size());
```

The `uncompress` function takes an array of `Bytef*` (defined in zlib's `zconf.h`) as the destination buffer; we are using an `std::vector` of `int` values and casting it to a `Bytef*` array. The second parameter is the total size of the destination buffer, in our case we are using a `vector` of `int` values making the total size the number of rows x the number of columns x the size of an `int`; or `m_width * m_height * sizeof(int)`. We then pass in our decoded string and its size as the final two parameters. Our `ids` vector now contains all of our tile IDs and the function moves on to set the size of our data vector for us to fill with our tile IDs:

```
std::vector<int> layerRow(m_width);
for(int j = 0; j < m_height; j++)
{
   data.push_back(layerRow);
}
```

We can now fill our data array with the correct values:

```
for(int rows = 0; rows < m_height; rows++)
{
   for(int cols = 0; cols < m_width; cols++)
   {
      data[rows][cols] = ids[rows * m_width + cols];
   }
}
```

And finally we set this layer's tile data and then push the layer into the layers array of our `Level`.

We must now define the functions in our `Level.cpp` file.

Drawing the map

We are finally at a stage where we can start drawing our tiles to the screen. Inside the earlier created `TileLayer.cpp` file we will now need to define our functions for the layer. Starting with the constructor:

```
TileLayer::TileLayer(int tileSize, const
  std::vector<Tileset> &tilesets) : m_tileSize(tileSize),
  m_tilesets(tilesets), m_position(0,0), m_velocity(0,0)
{
  m_numColumns = (TheGame::Instance()->getGameWidth() /
    m_tileSize);
  m_numRows = (TheGame::Instance()->getGameHeight() / m_tileSize);
}
```

The new `Game::getGameWidth` and `Game::getGameHeight` functions are just simple getter functions that return variables set in the `Game::init` function:

```
int getGameWidth() const
{
  return m_gameWidth;
}
int getGameHeight() const
{
  return m_gameHeight;
}
```

The `TileLayer` update function uses `velocity` to set the map's position; we will cover this in more detail when we come to scroll our map:

```
void TileLayer::update()
{
  m_position += m_velocity;
}
```

The `render` function is where all the magic happens:

```
void TileLayer::render()
{
  int x, y, x2, y2 = 0;

  x = m_position.getX() / m_tileSize;
  y = m_position.getY() / m_tileSize;

  x2 = int(m_position.getX()) % m_tileSize;
  y2 = int(m_position.getY()) % m_tileSize;
```

Creating and Displaying Tile Maps

```
for(int i = 0; i < m_numRows; i++)
{
  for(int j = 0; j < m_numColumns; j++)
  {
      int id = m_tileIDs[i][j + x];

        if(id == 0)
        {
          continue;
        }

      Tileset tileset = getTilesetByID(id);

      id--;

      TheTextureManager::Instance()->drawTile(tileset.name, 2, 2,
      (j * m_tileSize) - x2, (i * m_tileSize) - y2, m_tileSize,
      m_tileSize, (id - (tileset.firstGridID - 1)) /
      tileset.numColumns, (id - (tileset.firstGridID - 1)) %
      tileset.numColumns, TheGame::Instance()->getRenderer());
  }
 }
}
```

You will notice that there is a new function in the `TextureManager`, `drawTile`. This function is specifically for drawing tiles and includes margin and spacing values. Here it is:

```
void TextureManager::drawTile(std::string id, int margin, int
  spacing, int x, int y, int width, int height, int currentRow,
    int currentFrame, SDL_Renderer *pRenderer)
{
  SDL_Rect srcRect;
  SDL_Rect destRect;
  srcRect.x = margin + (spacing + width) * currentFrame;
  srcRect.y = margin + (spacing + height) * currentRow;
  srcRect.w = destRect.w = width;
  srcRect.h = destRect.h = height;
  destRect.x = x;
  destRect.y = y;

  SDL_RenderCopyEx(pRenderer, m_textureMap[id], &srcRect,
    &destRect, 0, 0, SDL_FLIP_NONE);
}
```

Let's look closer at the `render` function; we will ignore the positioning code for now:

```
for(int i = 0; i < m_numRows; i++)
{
  for(int j = 0; j < m_numColumns; j++)
  {
    int id = m_tileIDs[i][j + x];

    if(id == 0)
    {
      continue;
    }

    Tilesettileset = getTilesetByID(id);

    id--;

    TheTextureManager::Instance()->drawTile(tileset.name,
    tileset.margin, tileset.spacing, (j * m_tileSize) - x2, (i *
    m_tileSize) - y2, m_tileSize, m_tileSize, (id -
    (tileset.firstGridID - 1)) / tileset.numColumns, (id -
    (tileset.firstGridID - 1)) % tileset.numColumns,
    TheGame::Instance()->getRenderer());
  }
}
```

We loop through the number of columns and the number of rows:

```
for(int i = 0; i < m_numRows; i++)
{
  for(int j = 0; j < m_numColumns; j++)
  {
```

This is not the number of rows and columns in the full tile ID array, it is actually the number of columns and rows needed to fill the size of our game. We do not want to be drawing anything that we do not have to. We obtained these values earlier in the constructor:

```
m_numColumns = (TheGame::Instance()->getGameWidth() / m_tileSize);
m_numRows = (TheGame::Instance()->getGameHeight() / m_tileSize);
```

Next we get the current tile ID from the array (ignore the `+ x` for now):

```
int id = m_tileIDs[i + y][j + x];
```

Creating and Displaying Tile Maps

We check if the tile ID is 0. If it is, then we do not want to draw anything:

```
if(id == 0)
{
  continue;
}
```

Otherwise we grab the correct tileset:

```
Tileset tileset = getTilesetByID(id);
```

Getting the tileset uses a very simple function, `getTilesetByID`, which compares each tileset's `firstgid` value and returns the correct tileset:

```
Tileset TileLayer::getTilesetByID(int tileID)
{
  for(int i = 0; i < m_tilesets.size(); i++)
  {
    if( i + 1 <= m_tilesets.size() - 1)
    {
      if(tileID >= m_tilesets[i].firstGridID&&tileID < m_tilesets[i +
        1].firstGridID)
      {
        return m_tilesets[i];
      }
    }
    else
    {
      return m_tilesets[i];
    }
  }

  std::cout << "did not find tileset, returning empty tileset\n";
  Tileset t;
  return t;
}
```

Next we move on to drawing the tiles:

```
id--;

TheTextureManager::Instance()->drawTile(tileset.name,
  tileset.margin, tileset.spacing, (j * m_tileSize) - x2, (i *
  m_tileSize) - y2, m_tileSize, m_tileSize, (id -
  (tileset.firstGridID - 1)) / tileset.numColumns, (id -
```

[178]

```
      (tileset.firstGridID - 1)) % tileset.numColumns,
        TheGame::Instance()->getRenderer());
    }
  }
}
```

First we decrement the ID so that we can draw the correct tile from the tilesheet, even if it is at position `0,0`. We then use the `drawTile` function to copy across the correct tile using the tileset we grabbed earlier, to set the first parameter of the function, which is the `name` of the texture. Again, we can use the tileset for the next two parameters, `margin` and `spacing`:

```
tileset.margin, tileset.spacing
```

The next two parameters set the position we want to draw our tiles at:

```
(j * m_tileSize) - x2, (i * m_tileSize) - y2
```

Ignoring the `x2` and `y2` values for now (they are 0 anyway), we can set the current `x` position as the current column multiplied by the width of a tile and the `y` value as the current row multiplied by the height of a tile. We then set the width and height of the tile we are copying across:

```
m_tileSize, m_tileSize,
```

And finally we work out the location of the tile on the tilesheet:

```
(id - (tileset.firstGridID - 1)) / tileset.numColumns,
(id - (tileset.firstGridID - 1)) % tileset.numColumns,
```

We subtract the `firstGridID - 1` to allow us to treat each tilesheet the same and obtain the correct location. For example, the `firstGridID` of a tileset could be 50 and the current tile ID could be 70. We know that this is actually going to be tile 19 (after we decrement the ID) on the tilesheet itself.

Finally, we must create a level in our `PlayState` class:

```
bool PlayState::onEnter()
{
  LevelParser levelParser;
  pLevel = levelParser.parseLevel("assets/map1.tmx");

  std::cout << "entering PlayState\n";
  return true;
}
```

Creating and Displaying Tile Maps

Next, draw it in the `render` function, and also do the same with the `update` function:

```
void PlayState::render()
{
  pLevel->render();
}
```

We will also have to comment out any functions that use objects (such as `collisionChecks`) as we don't have any yet and this will cause a runtime error. Run our game and you will see our tile map being drawn to the screen.

Scrolling a tile map

What we have created so far is fine for a game that takes place in one area that is the size of our window, but what about if we want to have large maps that are open to exploration. This is where scrolling comes into play. We have actually implemented this already but have not yet gone through it step-by-step or seen it in action. Let's do this now.

First of all, we must resize our map in the Tiled application. Navigating to **Map | Resize Map...** will allow us to do this. Leave the height of our map at 15 and change the width to 60. Fill up the remaining squares with whatever tiles you like. The map would then look like the following screenshot:

Save the map and we can look at the code:

```
int x, y, x2, y2 = 0;

x = m_position.getX() / m_tileSize;
y = m_position.getY() / m_tileSize;

x2 = int(m_position.getX()) % m_tileSize;
y2 = int(m_position.getY()) % m_tileSize;
```

When scrolling the map we don't actually move it more than a tile width; we use the position value to work out where we should begin drawing our map from within the tile ID array. To get the x value we can use the position we have moved to divided by the tile width. For example, let's say that we have moved the map to `x position = 100` and the tile width is 32; this would give us a value of 3.125, but since we are using `int` values, this will simply be 3. We now know that we are to start drawing from the third tile across on the map. The `y` position works in the same way.

To ensure that our tile drawing does not jump between tiles, but smoothly scrolls, we use a modulo calculation to get the remaining tile amount that we need to move by and use that to position our map:

```
x2 = int(m_position.getX()) % m_tileSize;
y2 = int(m_position.getY()) % m_tileSize;
```

We then subtract these values in the `draw` function:

```
(j * m_tileSize) - x2, (i * m_tileSize) - y2
```

We can test this by setting a velocity in our layers `update` function:

```
void TileLayer::update()
{
  m_position += m_velocity;
  m_velocity.setX(1);
}
```

And then in `PlayState` we can call this function:

```
void PlayState::update()
{
  pLevel->update();
}
```

Run the game and you will see the map scrolling. At the moment we have not put any kind of handling in for looping the map or stopping at the end. We will cover this when we begin to create a game in later chapters.

Parsing object layers

The final topic we will cover in this chapter is loading objects from our Tiled map file. This is extremely useful and takes the guesswork out of placing objects within a level. Open up the Tiled application and we can create our first **Object Layer** by clicking **Layer | Add Object Layer**. This will create a new layer called **Object Layer 1** as shown in the following screenshot:

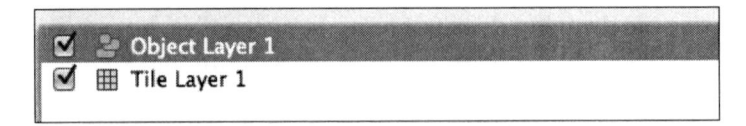

We can create objects and assign any values and properties we want on these layers. First we will create a rectangle. Press R and click anywhere on your tile map, you will see a small square appear, as shown in the following screenshot:

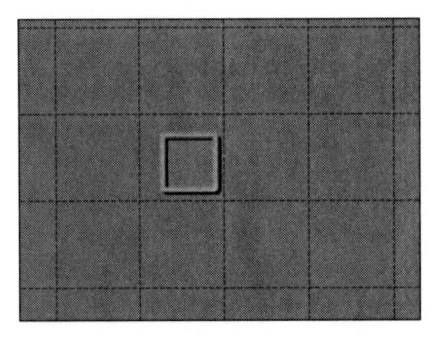

Right-click on this square and click on **Object Properties…**. This will bring up the object properties dialog as shown in the following screenshot:

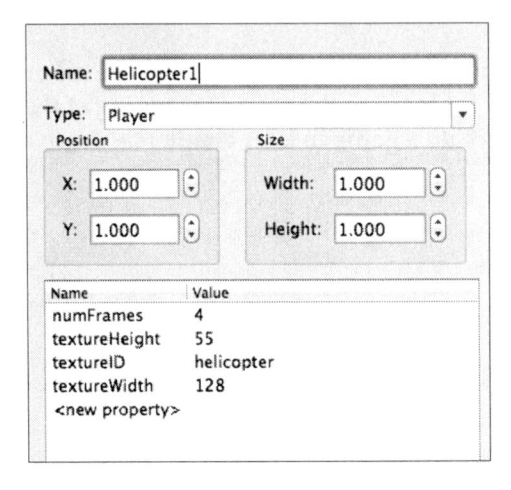

Here, we can set the values we want our object to have, just like our previous state XML files. Go ahead and fill in the dialog box as shown in the preceding screenshot. The positions and sizes of this dialog box deal in tiles, not pixels, so x = 1 is actually x = tile width and so on. Saving this map will add our new object layer to the map file:

```
<objectgroup name="Object Layer 1" width="60" height="15">
  <object name="Helicopter1" type="Player" x="32" y="32" width="32
    height="32">
    <properties>
      <property name="numFrames" value="4"/>
      <property name="textureHeight" value="55"/>
      <property name="textureID" value="helicopter"/>
      <property name="textureWidth" value="128"/>
    </properties>
  </object>
</objectgroup>
```

We are also going to use another property list to load in our textures for this map. **Map | Map Properties** will bring up the map properties dialog as shown in the following screenshot:

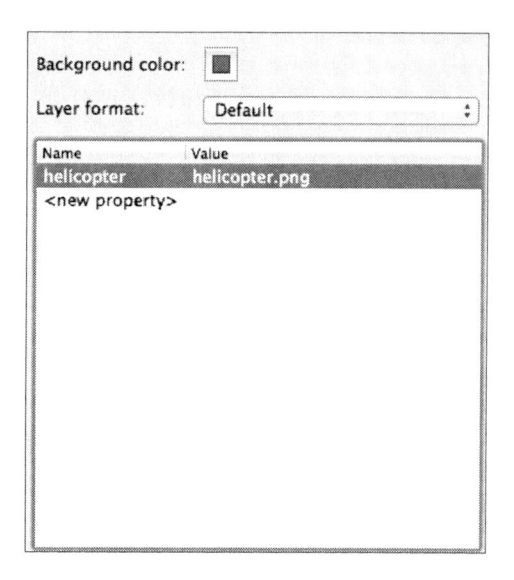

Here we can add the textures we need for this map's objects. The saved file will now have an additional property list for us to parse through:

```
<properties>
  <property name="helicopter" value="helicopter.png"/>
</properties>
```

Developing the ObjectLayer class

Back in our project we will now create a new layer type called `ObjectLayer`. Create `ObjectLayer.h` and we can add the following code:

```
class ObjectLayer : public Layer
{
  public:
  virtual void update();
  virtual void render();

  std::vector<GameObject*>* getGameObjects()
  {
    return &m_gameObjects;
  }

  private:

  std::vector<GameObject*> m_gameObjects;
};
```

We will also define these functions in `ObjectLayer.cpp`:

```
void ObjectLayer::update()
{
  for(int i = 0; i < m_gameObjects.size(); i++)
  {
    m_gameObjects[i]->update();
  }

}
void ObjectLayer::render()
{
  for(int i = 0; i < m_gameObjects.size(); i++)
  {
    m_gameObjects[i]->draw();
  }
}
```

Our `ObjectLayer` class is very simple. It only needs to draw and update the objects for that layer. Now let's parse our `ObjectLayer`. We will need two new functions in the `LevelParser` class:

```
void parseTextures(TiXmlElement* pTextureRoot);

void parseObjectLayer(TiXmlElement* pObjectElement,
    std::vector<Layer*> *pLayers);
```

The `parseLevel` function must now include these functions and pass in the correct XML node:

```
// we must parse the textures needed for this level, which have been
added to properties
for(TiXmlElement* e = pProperties->FirstChildElement(); e != NULL;
  e = e->NextSiblingElement())
{
  if(e->Value() == std::string("property"))
  {
  parseTextures(e);
  }
}
```

We will alter the way we were searching for tile layers to also search for object layers:

```
// parse any object layers
for(TiXmlElement* e = pRoot->FirstChildElement(); e != NULL; e =
  e->NextSiblingElement())
{
  if(e->Value() == std::string("objectgroup") || e->Value() ==
    std::string("layer"))
  {
    if(e->FirstChildElement()->Value() == std::string("object"))
    {
      parseObjectLayer(e, pLevel->getLayers());
    }
    else if(e->FirstChildElement()->Value() ==
        std::string("data"))
    {
      parseTileLayer(e, pLevel->getLayers(), pLevel->getTilesets());
    }
  }
}
```

Now we need to define the new functions; `parseTextures` is a very small and simple function:

```
void LevelParser::parseTextures(TiXmlElement* pTextureRoot)
{
  TheTextureManager::Instance()->load(pTextureRoot-
>Attribute("value"), pTextureRoot->Attribute("name"),
  TheGame::Instance()->getRenderer());
}
```

Creating and Displaying Tile Maps

It gets the texture values and adds them to the `TextureManager`. The `parseObjects` function is a little longer but not particularly complicated:

```
void LevelParser::parseObjectLayer(TiXmlElement* pObjectElement,
  std::vector<Layer*> *pLayers)
{
    // create an object layer
    ObjectLayer* pObjectLayer = new ObjectLayer();

    std::cout << pObjectElement->FirstChildElement()->Value();

    for(TiXmlElement* e = pObjectElement->FirstChildElement(); e !=
      NULL; e = e->NextSiblingElement())
      {
        std::cout << e->Value();
        if(e->Value() == std::string("object"))
        {
           int x, y, width, height, numFrames, callbackID, animSpeed;
           std::string textureID;

           // get the initial node values type, x and y
           e->Attribute("x", &x);
           e->Attribute("y", &y);
           GameObject* pGameObject =
              TheGameObjectFactory::Instance()->create(e-
>Attribute("type"));

           // get the property values
           for(TiXmlElement* properties = e->FirstChildElement();
              properties != NULL; properties = properties-
>NextSiblingElement())
              {
                 if(properties->Value() == std::string("properties"))
                 {
                    for(TiXmlElement* property = properties-
>FirstChildElement(); property != NULL; property = property-
>NextSiblingElement())
                       {
                          if(property->Value() == std::string("property"))
                          {
                             if(property->Attribute("name") ==
                                std::string("numFrames"))
                                {
                                   property->Attribute("value", &numFrames);
```

[186]

```cpp
                    }
                    else if(property->Attribute("name") ==
                      std::string("textureHeight"))
                    {
                      property->Attribute("value", &height);
                    }
                    else if(property->Attribute("name") ==
                      std::string("textureID"))
                    {
                      textureID = property->Attribute("value");
                    }
                    else if(property->Attribute("name") ==
                      std::string("textureWidth"))
                    {
                      property->Attribute("value", &width);
                    }
                    else if(property->Attribute("name") ==
                      std::string("callbackID"))
                    {
                      property->Attribute("value", &callbackID);
                    }
                    else if(e->Attribute("name") ==
                      std::string("animSpeed"))
                    {
                      property->Attribute("value", &animSpeed);
                    }
                  }
                }
              }
            }
            pGameObject->load(new
          LoaderParams(x, y, width, height, textureID,
          numFrames, callbackID, animSpeed));
          pObjectLayer->getGameObjects()->push_back(pGameObject);
        }
      }

    pLayers->push_back(pObjectLayer);
  }
```

[187]

Creating and Displaying Tile Maps

We load the object in a very similar way to the state parser, yet this time we must check for the `name` of the property rather than grabbing the `attribute` directly:

```
if(property->Attribute("name") == std::string("numFrames"))
{
   property->Attribute("value", &numFrames);
}
```

We can then create the object just like the state parser:

```
pGameObject->load(new
   LoaderParams(x,y,width,height,textureID,numFrames,callbackID,
   animSpeed));
```

And add it to this layer's game object array:

```
pObjectLayer->getGameObjects()->push_back(pGameObject);
```

Once we have loaded all of the objects for this layer, we can push it into our `Level` layer array:

```
pLayers->push_back(pObjectLayer);
```

Run the game and you will see our helicopter in the `PlayState` again.

Summary

We are getting closer to a fully-fledged game all the time. This chapter covered a quick way to create 2D maps through the use of tiles and also looked at using an external application to place objects within our levels. The next two chapters will tie up all of the remaining loose ends and we will create some actual games.

8
Creating Alien Attack

The framework has come on in leaps and bounds and we are almost ready to make our first game. We are going to create a simple 2D sidescrolling shooter in the vein of the classic '80's and '90's shooter games such as R-Type or Pulstar. However, the game will not be set in space. Aliens have attacked earth and only you and your weaponized helicopter can stop them. One level of fast-paced action is available in the source code downloads and this chapter will cover the steps taken to create it. Here is a screenshot of the game we will be creating:

Creating Alien Attack

And another slightly more hectic shot:

There are still a few things that the framework must handle before we can create this game. These additions include:

- Sound
- Collision detection

By the end of the chapter you will have a good understanding of how this game was built using the framework and you will have the ability to continue and improve it. In this chapter, we will cover:

- Implementing sound
- Creating game-specific object classes
- Shooting and detecting bullets
- Creating different enemy types
- Developing a game

Using the SDL_mixer extension for sound

The SDL_mixer extension has its own Mercurial repository that can be used to grab the latest source for the extension. It is located at `http://hg.libsdl.org/SDL_mixer`. The TortoiseHg application can again be used to clone the extension's Mercurial repository. Follow these steps to build the library:

1. Open up TortoiseHg and press *CTRL+SHIFT+N* to start cloning a new repository.
2. Type `http://hg.libsdl.org/SDL_mixer` into the source box.
3. The **Destination** will be `C:\SDL2_mixer`.
4. Hit **Clone** and wait for completion.
5. Navigate to `C:\SDL2_mixer\VisualC\` and open `SDL_mixer.vcproj` in Visual Studio 2010.
6. As long as the x64 folder outlined in *Chapter 2, Drawing in SDL* was created, the project will convert with no issues.
7. We are going to build the library without MP3 support as we are not going to need it, and also it does not work particularly well with SDL 2.0.
8. Add `MP3_MUSIC_DISABLED` to the **Preprocessor Definitions** in the project properties, which can be found by navigating to **C/C++ | Preprocessor**, and build as per the `SDL_image` instructions in *Chapter 2, Drawing in SDL*.

Creating the SoundManager class

The game created in this chapter will not need any advanced sound manipulation, meaning the `SoundManager` class is quite basic. The class has only been tested using the `.ogg` files for music and the `.wav` files for sound effects. Here is the header file:

```
enum sound_type
{
  SOUND_MUSIC = 0,
  SOUND_SFX = 1
};

class SoundManager
{
public:

  static SoundManager* Instance()
```

```cpp
    {
      if(s_pInstance == 0)
      {
        s_pInstance = newSoundManager();
        return s_pInstance;
      }
      return s_pInstance;
    }

    bool load(std::string fileName, std::string id, sound_type type);

    void playSound(std::string id, int loop);
    void playMusic(std::string id, int loop);

    private:

    static SoundManager* s_pInstance;

    std::map<std::string, Mix_Chunk*> m_sfxs;
    std::map<std::string, Mix_Music*> m_music;

    SoundManager();
    ~SoundManager();

    SoundManager(const SoundManager&);
    SoundManager &operator=(const SoundManager&);
};

typedef SoundManager TheSoundManager;
```

The `SoundManager` class is a singleton; this makes sense because there should only be one place that the sounds are stored and it should be accessible from anywhere in the game. Before sound can be used, `Mix_OpenAudio` must be called to set up the audio for the game. `Mix_OpenAudio` takes the following parameters:

```
(int frequency, Uint16 format, int channels, int chunksize)
```

This is done in the `SoundManager`'s constructor with values that will work well for most games.

```cpp
SoundManager::SoundManager()
{
  Mix_OpenAudio(22050, AUDIO_S16, 2, 4096);
}
```

Chapter 8

The `SoundManager` class stores sounds in two different `std::map` containers:

```
std::map<std::string, Mix_Chunk*> m_sfxs;
std::map<std::string, Mix_Music*> m_music;
```

These maps store pointers to one of two different types used by `SDL_mixer` (`Mix_Chunk*` and `Mix_Music*`), keyed using strings. The `Mix_Chunk*` types are used for sound effects and the `Mix_Music*` types are of course used for music. When loading a music file or a sound effect into `SoundManager`, we pass in the type of sound we are loading as an `enum` called `sound_type`.

```
bool load(std::string fileName, std::string id, sound_type type);
```

This type is then used to decide which `std::map` to add the loaded sound to and also which `load` function to use from `SDL_mixer`. The `load` function is defined in `SoundManager.cpp`.

```
bool SoundManager::load(std::string fileName, std::string id, sound_type type)
{
  if(type == SOUND_MUSIC)
  {
    Mix_Music* pMusic = Mix_LoadMUS(fileName.c_str());

    if(pMusic == 0)
    {
      std::cout << "Could not load music: ERROR - "
      << Mix_GetError() << std::endl;
      return false;
    }

    m_music[id] = pMusic;
    return true;
  }
  else if(type == SOUND_SFX)
  {
    Mix_Chunk* pChunk = Mix_LoadWAV(fileName.c_str());
    if(pChunk == 0)
    {
      std::cout << "Could not load SFX: ERROR - "
      << Mix_GetError() << std::endl;

      return false;
    }

    m_sfxs[id] = pChunk;
    return true;
  }
  return false;
}
```

Once a sound has been loaded it can be played using the `playSound` or `playMusic` functions:

```
void playSound(std::string id, int loop);
void playMusic(std::string id, int loop);
```

Both of these functions take the ID of the sound to be played and the amount of times that it is to be looped. Both functions are very similar.

```
void SoundManager::playMusic(std::string id, int loop)
{
  Mix_PlayMusic(m_music[id], loop);
}

void SoundManager::playSound(std::string id, int loop)
{
  Mix_PlayChannel(-1, m_sfxs[id], loop);
}
```

One difference between `Mix_PlayMusic` and `Mix_PlayChannel` is that the latter takes an `int` as the first parameter; this is the channel that the sound is to be played on. A value of `-1` (as seen in the preceding code) tells `SDL_mixer` to play the sound on any available channel.

Finally, when the `SoundManager` class is destroyed, it will call `Mix_CloseAudio`:

```
SoundManager::~SoundManager()
{
  Mix_CloseAudio();
}
```

And that's it for the `SoundManager` class.

Setting up the basic game objects

The majority of the work that went into creating Alien Attack was done in the object classes, while almost everything else was already being handled by manager classes in the framework. Here are the most important changes:

GameObject revamped

The `GameObject` base class has a lot more to it than it previously did.

```
class GameObject
{
public:
```

```cpp
    // base class needs virtual destructor
    virtual ~GameObject() {}
    // load from file
    virtual void load(std::unique_ptr<LoaderParams> const &pParams)=0;
    // draw the object
    virtual void draw()=0;
    // do update stuff
    virtual void update()=0;
    // remove anything that needs to be deleted
    virtual void clean()=0;
    // object has collided, handle accordingly
    virtual void collision() = 0;
    // get the type of the object
    virtual std::string type() = 0;
    // getters for common variables
    Vector2D& getPosition() { return m_position; }
    int getWidth() { return m_width; }
    int getHeight() { return m_height; }
    // scroll along with tile map
    void scroll(float scrollSpeed) { m_position.setX(m_position.getX() -
    scrollSpeed); }
    // is the object currently being updated?
    bool updating() { return m_bUpdating; }
    // is the object dead?
    bool dead() { return m_bDead; }
    // is the object doing a death animation?
    bool dying() { return m_bDying; }
    // set whether to update the object or not
    void setUpdating(bool updating) { m_bUpdating = updating; }

protected:

    // constructor with default initialisation list
    GameObject() :  m_position(0,0),
    m_velocity(0,0),
    m_acceleration(0,0),
    m_width(0),
    m_height(0),
    m_currentRow(0),
    m_currentFrame(0),
    m_bUpdating(false),
    m_bDead(false),
    m_bDying(false),
    m_angle(0),
```

```cpp
    m_alpha(255)
    {
    }
    // movement variables
    Vector2D m_position;
    Vector2D m_velocity;
    Vector2D m_acceleration;
    // size variables
    int m_width;
    int m_height;
    // animation variables
    int m_currentRow;
    int m_currentFrame;
    int m_numFrames;
    std::string m_textureID;
    // common boolean variables
    bool m_bUpdating;
    bool m_bDead;
    bool m_bDying;
    // rotation
    double m_angle;
    // blending
    int m_alpha;
};
```

This class now has a lot of the member variables that used to be in `SDLGameObject`. New variables for checking whether an object is updating, doing the death animation, or is dead, have been added. Updating is set to true when an object is within the game screen after scrolling with the game level.

In place of a regular pointer to `LoaderParams` in the load function, an `std::unique_ptr` pointer is now used; this is part of the new **C++11 standard** and ensures that the pointer is deleted after going out of scope.

```cpp
virtual void load(std::unique_ptr<LoaderParams> const &pParams)=0;
```

There are two new functions that each derived object must now implement (whether it's owned or inherited):

```cpp
// object has collided, handle accordingly
virtual void collision() = 0;

// get the type of the object
virtual std::string type() = 0;
```

SDLGameObject is now ShooterObject

The `SDLGameObject` class has now been renamed to `ShooterObject` and is a lot more specific to this type of game:

```
class ShooterObject : public GameObject
{
public:

  virtual ~ShooterObject() {}// for polymorphism
  virtual void load(std::unique_ptr<LoaderParams> const
  &pParams);
  virtual void draw();
  virtual void update();
  virtual void clean() {}// not implemented in this class
  virtual void collision() {}//not implemented in this class
  virtual std::string type() { return "SDLGameObject"; }

protected:

  // we won't directly create ShooterObject's
  ShooterObject();

  // draw the animation for the object being destroyed
  void doDyingAnimation();

  // how fast will this object fire bullets? with a counter
  int m_bulletFiringSpeed;
  int m_bulletCounter;

  // how fast will this object move?
  int m_moveSpeed;

  // how long will the death animation takes? with a counter
  int m_dyingTime;
  int m_dyingCounter;

  // has the explosion sound played?
  bool m_bPlayedDeathSound;
};
```

Creating Alien Attack

This class has default implementations for draw and update that can be used in derived classes; they are essentially the same as the previous `SDLGameObject` class, so we will not cover them here. A new function that has been added is `doDyingAnimation`. This function is responsible for updating the animation when enemies explode and then setting them to dead so that they can be removed from the game.

```
void ShooterObject::doDyingAnimation()
{
  // keep scrolling with the map
  scroll(TheGame::Instance()->getScrollSpeed());

  m_currentFrame = int(((SDL_GetTicks() / (1000 / 3)) %
  m_numFrames));

  if(m_dyingCounter == m_dyingTime)
  {
    m_bDead = true;
  }
  m_dyingCounter++; //simple counter, fine with fixed frame rate
}
```

Player inherits from ShooterObject

The **Player** object now inherits from the new `ShooterObject` class and implements its own update function. Some new game-specific functions and variables have been added:

```
private:

  // bring the player back if there are lives left
  void ressurect();

  // handle any input from the keyboard, mouse, or joystick
  void handleInput();

  // handle any animation for the player
  void handleAnimation();

  // player can be invulnerable for a time
  int m_invulnerable;
  int m_invulnerableTime;
  int m_invulnerableCounter;
};
```

The `ressurect` function resets the player back to the center of the screen and temporarily makes the `Player` object invulnerable; this is visualized using `alpha` of the texture. This function is also responsible for resetting the size value of the texture which is changed in `doDyingAnimation` to accommodate for the explosion texture:

```
void Player::ressurect()
{
  TheGame::Instance()->setPlayerLives(TheGame::Instance()
  ->getPlayerLives() - 1);

  m_position.setX(10);
  m_position.setY(200);
  m_bDying = false;

  m_textureID = "player";

  m_currentFrame = 0;
  m_numFrames = 5;
  m_width = 101;
  m_height = 46;

  m_dyingCounter = 0;
  m_invulnerable = true;
}
```

Animation is a big part of the feel of the `Player` object; from flashing (when invulnerable), to rotating (when moving in a forward or backward direction). This has led to there being a separate function dedicated to handling animation:

```
void Player::handleAnimation()
{
  // if the player is invulnerable we can flash its alpha to let
  people know
  if(m_invulnerable)
  {
    // invulnerability is finished, set values back
    if(m_invulnerableCounter == m_invulnerableTime)
    {
      m_invulnerable = false;
      m_invulnerableCounter = 0;
      m_alpha = 255;
    }
    else// otherwise, flash the alpha on and off
    {
      if(m_alpha == 255)
      {
```

Creating Alien Attack

```
      m_alpha = 0;
    }
    else
    {
      m_alpha = 255;
    }
  }

  // increment our counter
  m_invulnerableCounter++;
}

// if the player is not dead then we can change the angle with
// the velocity to give the impression of a moving helicopter
if(!m_bDead)
{
  if(m_velocity.getX() < 0)
  {
    m_angle = -10.0;
  }
  else if(m_velocity.getX() > 0)
  {
    m_angle = 10.0;
  }
  else
  {
    m_angle = 0.0;
  }
}

// our standard animation code - for helicopter propellors
m_currentFrame = int(((SDL_GetTicks() / (100)) % m_numFrames));
}
```

The angle and `alpha` of an object are changed using new parameters to the `drawFrame` function of `TextureManager`:

```
void TextureManager::drawFrame(std::string id, int x, int y, int
width, int height, int currentRow, int currentFrame, SDL_Renderer
*pRenderer, double angle, int alpha, SDL_RendererFlip flip)
{
  SDL_Rect srcRect;
  SDL_Rect destRect;
  srcRect.x = width * currentFrame;
  srcRect.y = height * currentRow;
```

```
    srcRect.w = destRect.w = width;
    srcRect.h = destRect.h = height;
    destRect.x = x;
    destRect.y = y;

    // set the alpha of the texture and pass in the angle
    SDL_SetTextureAlphaMod(m_textureMap[id], alpha);
    SDL_RenderCopyEx(pRenderer, m_textureMap[id], &srcRect,
    &destRect, angle, 0, flip);
}
```

Finally the `Player::update` function ties this all together while also having extra logic to handle when a level is complete:

```
void Player::update()
{
  // if the level is complete then fly off the screen
  if(TheGame::Instance()->getLevelComplete())
  {
    if(m_position.getX() >= TheGame::Instance()->getGameWidth())
    {
      TheGame::Instance()->setCurrentLevel(TheGame::Instance()
      ->getCurrentLevel() + 1);
    }
    else
    {
      m_velocity.setY(0);
      m_velocity.setX(3);
      ShooterObject::update();
      handleAnimation();
    }
  }
  else
  {
    // if the player is not doing its death animation then update
    it normally
    if(!m_bDying)
    {
      // reset velocity
      m_velocity.setX(0);
      m_velocity.setY(0);

      // get input
      handleInput();
      // do normal position += velocity update
```

Creating Alien Attack

```
    ShooterObject::update();

  // update the animation
  handleAnimation();
}
else // if the player is doing the death animation
{
  m_currentFrame = int(((SDL_GetTicks() / (100)) %
  m_numFrames));

  // if the death animation has completed
  if(m_dyingCounter == m_dyingTime)
  {
    // ressurect the player
    ressurect();
  }

  m_dyingCounter++;
    }
   }
  }
}
```

Once a level is complete and the player has flown offscreen, the `Player::update` function also tells the game to increment the current level:

```
TheGame::Instance()->setCurrentLevel(TheGame::Instance()-
>getCurrentLevel() + 1);
```

The `Game::setCurrentLevel` function changes the state to `BetweenLevelState`:

```
void Game::setCurrentLevel(int currentLevel)
{
  m_currentLevel = currentLevel;
  m_pGameStateMachine->changeState(new BetweenLevelState());
  m_bLevelComplete = false;
}
```

Lots of enemy types

A game such as Alien Attack needs a lot of enemy types to keep things interesting; each with its own behavior. Enemies should be easy to create and automatically added to the collision detection list. With this in mind, the `Enemy` class has now become a base class:

```
// Enemy base class
class Enemy : public ShooterObject
{
```

```
public:
  virtual std::string type() { return"Enemy"; }
protected:
  int m_health;

  Enemy() : ShooterObject() {}
  virtual ~Enemy() {} // for polymorphism
};
```

All enemy types will derive from this class, but it is important that they do not override the `type` method. The reason for this will become clear once we move onto our games collision detection classes. Go ahead and take a look at the enemy types in the Alien Attack source code to see how simple they are to create.

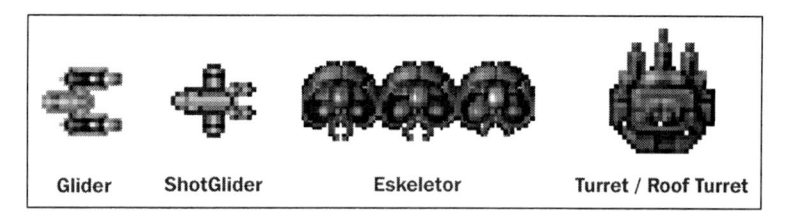

Glider   ShotGlider   Eskeletor   Turret / Roof Turret

Adding a scrolling background

Scrolling backgrounds are important to 2D games like this; they help give an illusion of depth and movement. This `ScrollingBackground` class uses two destination rectangles and two source rectangles; one expands while the other contracts. Once the expanding rectangle has reached its full width, both rectangles are reset and the loop continues:

```
void ScrollingBackground::load(std::unique_ptr<LoaderParams> const
&pParams)
{
  ShooterObject::load(std::move(pParams));
  m_scrollSpeed = pParams->getAnimSpeed();

  m_scrollSpeed = 1;

  m_srcRect1.x = 0;
  m_destRect1.x = m_position.getX();
  m_srcRect1.y = 0;
  m_destRect1.y = m_position.getY();

  m_srcRect1.w = m_destRect1.w = m_srcRect2Width =
  m_destRect1Width = m_width;
```

Creating Alien Attack

```
    m_srcRect1.h = m_destRect1.h = m_height;

  m_srcRect2.x = 0;
  m_destRect2.x = m_position.getX() + m_width;
  m_srcRect2.y = 0;
  m_destRect2.y = m_position.getY();

  m_srcRect2.w = m_destRect2.w = m_srcRect2Width =
  m_destRect2Width = 0;
  m_srcRect2.h = m_destRect2.h = m_height;
}

void ScrollingBackground::draw()
{
  // draw first rect
  SDL_RenderCopyEx(TheGame::Instance()->getRenderer(),
  TheTextureManager::Instance()->getTextureMap()[m_textureID],
  &m_srcRect1, &m_destRect1, 0, 0, SDL_FLIP_NONE);

  // draw second rect
  SDL_RenderCopyEx(TheGame::Instance()->getRenderer(),
  TheTextureManager::Instance()->getTextureMap()[m_textureID],
  &m_srcRect2, &m_destRect2, 0, 0, SDL_FLIP_NONE);

}

void ScrollingBackground::update()
{
  if(count == maxcount)
  {
    // make first rectangle smaller
    m_srcRect1.x += m_scrollSpeed;
    m_srcRect1.w -= m_scrollSpeed;
    m_destRect1.w -= m_scrollSpeed;

    // make second rectangle bigger
    m_srcRect2.w += m_scrollSpeed;
    m_destRect2.w += m_scrollSpeed;
    m_destRect2.x -= m_scrollSpeed;

    // reset and start again
    if(m_destRect2.w >= m_width)
    {
      m_srcRect1.x = 0;
```

```
            m_destRect1.x = m_position.getX();
            m_srcRect1.y = 0;
            m_destRect1.y = m_position.getY();

            m_srcRect1.w = m_destRect1.w = m_srcRect2Width =
            m_destRect1Width = m_width;
            m_srcRect1.h = m_destRect1.h = m_height;

            m_srcRect2.x = 0;
            m_destRect2.x = m_position.getX() + m_width;
            m_srcRect2.y = 0;
            m_destRect2.y = m_position.getY();

            m_srcRect2.w = m_destRect2.w = m_srcRect2Width =
            m_destRect2Width = 0;
            m_srcRect2.h = m_destRect2.h = m_height;
        }
        count = 0;
    }

    count++;
}
```

Handling bullets

Most objects in the game fire bullets and they all pretty much need to be checked for collisions against bullets as well; the bottom line—bullets are important in Alien Attack. The game has a dedicated `BulletHandler` class that handles the creation, destruction, updating, and rendering of bullets.

Two types of bullets

There are two types of bullets in the game, `PlayerBullet` and `EnemyBullet`, both of which are handled in the same `BulletManager` class. Both of the bullet classes are declared and defined in `Bullet.h`:

```
class PlayerBullet : public ShooterObject
{
public:

    PlayerBullet() : ShooterObject()
    {
```

Creating Alien Attack

```cpp
    }

    virtual ~PlayerBullet() {}

    virtual std::string type() { return "PlayerBullet"; }

    virtual void load(std::unique_ptr<LoaderParams> pParams, Vector2D
    heading)
    {
      ShooterObject::load(std::move(pParams));
      m_heading = heading;
    }

    virtual void draw()
    {
      ShooterObject::draw();
    }

    virtual void collision()
    {
      m_bDead = true;
    }

    virtual void update()
    {
      m_velocity.setX(m_heading.getX());
      m_velocity.setY(m_heading.getY());

      ShooterObject::update();
    }

    virtual void clean()
    {
      ShooterObject::clean();
    }

  private:

    Vector2D m_heading;
};

// Enemy Bullet is just a Player Bullet with a different typename
class EnemyBullet : public PlayerBullet
```

```
{
public:

    EnemyBullet() : PlayerBullet()
    {
    }

    virtual ~EnemyBullet() {}

    virtual std::string type() { return "EnemyBullet"; }
};
```

Bullets are very simple, they just move in one direction and at a certain speed.

The BulletHandler class

The `BulletHandler` class uses two public functions to add bullets:

```
void addPlayerBullet(int x, int y, int width, int height,
std::string textureID, int numFrames, Vector2D heading);
void addEnemyBullet(int x, int y, int width, int height,
std::string textureID, int numFrames, Vector2D heading);
```

The `BulletHandler` class is also a singleton. So, if an object wants to add a bullet to the game, it can do so using one of the above functions. Here is an example from the `ShotGlider` class:

```
TheBulletHandler::Instance()->addEnemyBullet(m_position.getX(),
m_position.getY() + 15, 16, 16, "bullet2", 1, Vector2D(-10, 0));
```

This will add a bullet at the current location of `ShotGlider`, with a heading vector of *V*(-10,0).

Both `add` functions are very similar; they create a new instance of `PlayerBullet` or `EnemyBullet` and then push it into the correct vector. Here are their definitions:

```
void BulletHandler::addPlayerBullet(int x, int y, int width, int
   height, std::string textureID, int numFrames, Vector2D heading)
{
   PlayerBullet* pPlayerBullet = newPlayerBullet();
   pPlayerBullet->load(std::unique_ptr<LoaderParams>(new
   LoaderParams(x, y, width, height, textureID, numFrames)),
   heading);
```

Creating Alien Attack

```cpp
    m_playerBullets.push_back(pPlayerBullet);
}

void BulletHandler::addEnemyBullet(int x, int y, int width, int
height, std::string textureID, int numFrames, Vector2D heading)
{
  EnemyBullet* pEnemyBullet = new EnemyBullet();
  pEnemyBullet->load(std::unique_ptr<LoaderParams>(new
  LoaderParams(x, y, width, height, textureID, numFrames)),
  heading);

  m_enemyBullets.push_back(pEnemyBullet);
}
```

A big advantage of having a separate place to store bullets like this, rather than have objects themselves manage their own bullets, is that there is no need to pass objects around just to get their bullets to check collisions against. This `BulletHandler` class gives us a centralized location that we can then easily pass to the collision handler.

The `update` and `draw` functions are essentially just loops that call each bullet's respective functions, however the `update` function will also destroy any bullets that have gone off the screen:

```cpp
    for (std::vector<PlayerBullet*>::iterator p_it =
    m_playerBullets.begin(); p_it != m_playerBullets.end();)
    {
      if((*p_it)->getPosition().getX() < 0 || (*p_it)
      ->getPosition().getX() >TheGame::Instance()->getGameWidth()
      || (*p_it)->getPosition().getY() < 0 || (*p_it)->
      getPosition().getY() >TheGame::Instance()->getGameHeight() ||
      (*p_it)->dead())// if off screen or dead
      {
        delete * p_it; // delete the bullet
        p_it = m_playerBullets.erase(p_it); //remove
      }
      else// continue to update and loop
      {
        (*p_it)->update();
        ++p_it;
      }
    }
```

Dealing with collisions

With so many bullets flying around and having the `Enemy` objects to check collisions against, it is important that there be a separate class that does this collision checking for us. This way we know where to look if we decide we want to implement a new way of checking for collisions or optimize the current code. The `Collision.h` file contains a static method that checks for collisions between two `SDL_Rect` objects:

```cpp
const static int s_buffer = 4;

static bool RectRect(SDL_Rect* A, SDL_Rect* B)
{
  int aHBuf = A->h / s_buffer;
  int aWBuf = A->w / s_buffer;

  int bHBuf = B->h / s_buffer;
  int bWBuf = B->w / s_buffer;

  // if the bottom of A is less than the top of B - no collision
  if((A->y + A->h) - aHBuf <= B->y + bHBuf)    { return false; }

  // if the top of A is more than the bottom of B = no collision
  if(A->y + aHBuf >= (B->y + B->h) - bHBuf)    { return false; }

  // if the right of A is less than the left of B - no collision
  if((A->x + A->w) - aWBuf <= B->x +  bWBuf)   { return false; }

  // if the left of A is more than the right of B - no collision
  if(A->x + aWBuf >= (B->x + B->w) - bWBuf)    { return false; }

  // otherwise there has been a collision
  return true;
}
```

The function makes use of a buffer, which is a value that is used to make the rectangles slightly smaller. In a game such as Alien Attack, exact collision on bounding rectangles would be slightly unfair and also not much fun. With the buffer value, more direct hits are needed before they will be registered as a collision. Here the buffer is set to 4; this will take a fourth off of each side of the rectangle.

The `Player` class will not handle its own collisions. This requires a way to separate out the player from the rest of the `GameObject` instants when the level is loaded. The `Level` class now stores a pointer to `Player`:

```cpp
Player* m_pPlayer;
```

Creating Alien Attack

With a public getter and setter:

```
Player* getPlayer() { return m_pPlayer; }
void setPlayer(Player* pPlayer) { m_pPlayer = pPlayer; }
```

The `LevelParser` instance sets this pointer when it loads in `Player` from the level file:

```
pGameObject->load(std::unique_ptr<LoaderParams>(new LoaderParams(x,
y, width, height, textureID, numFrames,callbackID, animSpeed)));

if(type == "Player") // check if it's the player
{
  pLevel->setPlayer(dynamic_cast<Player*>(pGameObject));
}

pObjectLayer->getGameObjects()->push_back(pGameObject);
```

Another addition to `Level` is that it holds a separate `std::vector` of `TileLayer*` which are tile layers that the game will check against for collisions. This value is passed in from the `.tmx` file and any `TileLayer` that needs to be checked for collisions must set `collidable` as a property in the tiled application.

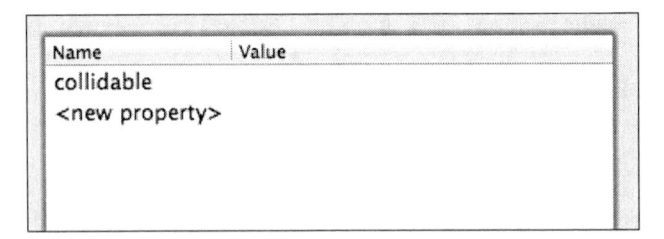

Name	Value
collidable	
<new property>	

This also requires a slight alteration in `LevelParser::parseLevel` when checking for object layers, just in case the layer does contain properties (in which case data would no longer be the first child element):

```
else if(e->FirstChildElement()->Value() == std::string("data") ||
(e->FirstChildElement()->NextSiblingElement() != 0 && e-
>FirstChildElement()->NextSiblingElement()->Value() ==
std::string("data")))
{
  parseTileLayer(e, pLevel->getLayers(), pLevel->getTilesets(),
  pLevel->getCollisionLayers());
}
```

The `LevelParser` instance can now add collision layers to the collision layers array in `parseTileLayer`:

```
// local temporary variable
bool collidable = false;

// other code...

for(TiXmlElement* e = pTileElement->FirstChildElement(); e !=
NULL; e = e->NextSiblingElement())
{
  if(e->Value() == std::string("properties"))
  {
    for(TiXmlElement* property = e->FirstChildElement(); property
    != NULL; property = property->NextSiblingElement())
    {
      if(property->Value() == std::string("property"))
      {
        if(property->Attribute("name") ==
        std::string("collidable"))
        {
          collidable = true;
        }
      }
    }
  }

  if(e->Value() == std::string("data"))
  {
    pDataNode = e;
  }
}

// other code...

// push into collision array if necessary
if(collidable)
{
  pCollisionLayers->push_back(pTileLayer);
}

pLayers->push_back(pTileLayer);
```

Creating a CollisionManager class

The class responsible for checking and handling all of these collisions is the `CollisionManager` class. Here is its declaration:

```
class CollisionManager
{
public:

  void checkPlayerEnemyBulletCollision(Player* pPlayer);
  void checkPlayerEnemyCollision(Player* pPlayer, const
  std::vector<GameObject*> &objects);
  void checkEnemyPlayerBulletCollision(const
  std::vector<GameObject*> &objects);
  void checkPlayerTileCollision(Player* pPlayer, const
  std::vector<TileLayer*> &collisionLayers);
};
```

Looking at the source code you will see that these functions are pretty big, yet they are relatively simple. They loop through each object that requires a collision test, create a rectangle for each, and then pass it to the static `RectRect` function defined in `Collision.h`. If a collision occurred then it calls the `collision` function for that object. The `checkEnemyPlayerBulletCollision` and `checkPlayerEnemyCollision` functions perform an extra check to see if the object is actually of `Enemy` type:

```
if(objects[i]->type() != std::string("Enemy") || !objects[i]-
>updating())
{
 continue;
}
```

If it is not, then it does not check the collision. This is why it is important that the `Enemy` subtypes do not override the `type` function or if they do, their type must also be added to this check. This condition also checks whether the object is updating or not; if it is not, then it is offscreen and does not need to be checked against for collision.

Checking for collision against tiles requires a similar method to working out where to start drawing the tiles from, which was implemented in the `TileLayer::render` function. Here is the `checkPlayerTileCollision` definition:

```
void CollisionManager::checkPlayerTileCollision(Player* pPlayer,
  const std::vector<TileLayer*> &collisionLayers)
{
  // iterate through collision layers
  for(std::vector<TileLayer*>::const_iterator it =
```

```
      collisionLayers.begin(); it != collisionLayers.end(); ++it)
    {
      TileLayer* pTileLayer = (*it);
      std::vector<std::vector<int>> tiles = pTileLayer-
      >getTileIDs();

      // get this layers position
      Vector2D layerPos = pTileLayer->getPosition();

      int x, y, tileColumn, tileRow, tileid = 0;

      // calculate position on tile map
      x = layerPos.getX() / pTileLayer->getTileSize();
      y = layerPos.getY() / pTileLayer->getTileSize();

      // if moving forward or upwards
      if(pPlayer->getVelocity().getX() >= 0 || pPlayer-
      >getVelocity().getY() >= 0)
      {
        tileColumn = ((pPlayer->getPosition().getX() + pPlayer-
        >getWidth()) / pTileLayer->getTileSize());
        tileRow = ((pPlayer->getPosition().getY() + pPlayer-
        >getHeight())
        / pTileLayer->getTileSize());
        tileid = tiles[tileRow + y][tileColumn + x];
      }
      else if(pPlayer->getVelocity().getX() < 0 || pPlayer-
      >getVelocity().getY() < 0) // if moving backwards or downwards
      {
        tileColumn = pPlayer->getPosition().getX() / pTileLayer-
        >getTileSize();
        tileRow = pPlayer->getPosition().getY() / pTileLayer-
        >getTileSize();
        tileid = tiles[tileRow + y][tileColumn + x];
      }
      if(tileid != 0) // if the tile id not blank then collide
      {
        pPlayer->collision();
      }
    }
  }
```

Possible improvements

Alien Attack is a pretty robust game at the moment; we highly recommend looking through the source code and becoming familiar with every aspect of it. Once you have a good understanding of most of the areas of the game, it is a lot easier to see where certain areas could be enhanced. Here are some ideas that could be added to improve the game:

- Bullets could be created at the start of a level and stored in an object pool; so rather than creating and deleting bullets all the time they can be pulled from and put back into the object pool. The main advantage of this approach is that the creation and destruction of objects can be quite expensive when it comes to performance. Eliminating this while the game is running could give a real performance boost.
- Collision detection could be optimized further, possibly through the addition of a **Quadtree** to stop unnecessary collision checks.
- The source code has a few areas that use string comparisons to check types. This can be a bit of a performance hog, so other options such as using `enums` as types may be a better option.

You may have noticed areas yourself that you feel you could improve upon. Working on these within the context of a game, where you can test the results, is a great learning experience.

Summary

The framework has been successfully used to create a game—Alien Attack. Throughout this chapter, the most important parts of the game were covered, along with a short explanation of why they were designed in such a way. With the source code for this game available, there is now a great project to start practicing with.

9
Creating Conan the Caveman

In the previous chapter, the creation of Alien Attack demonstrated that the framework is now at a point where it can be used to quickly create a 2D side scrolling shooter. Other genres are also simple to make with most of the changes once again being contained within the object classes.

In this chapter, we will cover:

- Adapting the previous code base for a new game
- More precise tile-collision detection
- Handling jumping
- Possible additions to the framework

This chapter will use the framework to create a platform game, Conan the Caveman. Here is a screenshot of the finished game level:

Here's another screenshot with more enemies:

As with the previous chapter, this chapter is not a step-by-step guide to creating Conan the Caveman, rather it is an overview of the most important aspects of the game. The project for the game is available in the source code downloads.

Setting up the basic game objects

In some ways this game is more complicated than Alien Attack, whereas in other ways it is simpler. This section will cover the changes that were made to the Alien Attack source code: what was altered, what was removed, and what was added.

No more bullets or bullet collisions

Conan the Caveman does not use projectile weapons, and therefore, there is no longer a `Bullet` class and the `CollisonManager` class no longer needs to have a function that checks for collisions between them; it only checks for the `Player` and `Enemy` collisions:

```
class CollisionManager
{
public:

    void checkPlayerEnemyCollision(Player* pPlayer, const
    std::vector<GameObject*>&objects);
};
```

Game objects and map collisions

Almost all objects will need to collide with the tile map and react accordingly. The `GameObject` class now has a private member that is a pointer to the collision layers; previously only the `Player` class had this variable:

```
std::vector<TileLayer*>* m_pCollisionLayers;
```

`GameObject` also now has a function to set this variable:

```
void setCollisionLayers(std::vector<TileLayer*>* layers) { m_pCollisionLayers = layers; }
```

The `Player` class would previously have this set at the end of the `LevelParser::parseLevel` function, as follows:

```
pLevel->getPlayer()->setCollisionLayers(pLevel->getCollisionLayers());
```

This is no longer needed, as each `GameObject` gets their `m_pCollisionLayers` variables set on creation in the object-layer parsing:

```
// load the object
pGameObject->load(std::unique_ptr<LoaderParams>(new LoaderParams(x, y, width, height, textureID, numFrames,callbackID, animSpeed)));
// set the collision layers
pGameObject->setCollisionLayers(pLevel->getCollisionLayers());
```

ShooterObject is now PlatformerObject

The shooter-specific code from Alien Attack has been stripped out of `ShooterObject` and the class is renamed to `PlatformerObject`. Anything that all game objects for this game will make use of is within this class:

```
class PlatformerObject : public GameObject
{
public:

  virtual ~PlatformerObject() {}

  virtual void load(std::unique_ptr<LoaderParams> const &pParams);

  virtual void draw();
  virtual void update();

  virtual void clean() {}
  virtual void collision() {}
```

Creating Conan the Caveman

```cpp
    virtual std::string type() { return "SDLGameObject"; }

  protected:

    PlatformerObject();

    bool checkCollideTile(Vector2D newPos);

    void doDyingAnimation();

    int m_bulletFiringSpeed;
    int m_bulletCounter;
    int m_moveSpeed;

    // how long the death animation takes, along with a counter
    int m_dyingTime;
    int m_dyingCounter;

    // has the explosion sound played?
    bool m_bPlayedDeathSound;

    bool m_bFlipped;

    bool m_bMoveLeft;
    bool m_bMoveRight;
    bool m_bRunning;

    bool m_bFalling;
    bool m_bJumping;
    bool m_bCanJump;

    Vector2D m_lastSafePos;

    int m_jumpHeight;
};
```

There are some variables and functions from Alien Attack that are still useful, plus a few new functions. One of the most important additions is the `checkCollideTile` function, which takes `Vector2D` as a parameter and checks whether it causes a collision:

```cpp
bool PlatformerObject::checkCollideTile(Vector2D newPos)
{
  if(newPos.m_y + m_height >= TheGame::Instance()->getGameHeight()
    - 32)
```

```
    {
      return false;
    }
    else
    {
      for(std::vector<TileLayer*>::iterator it = m_pCollisionLayers
      ->begin(); it != m_pCollisionLayers->end(); ++it)
      {
        TileLayer* pTileLayer = (*it);
        std::vector<std::vector<int>> tiles = pTileLayer
        ->getTileIDs();

        Vector2D layerPos = pTileLayer->getPosition();

        int x, y, tileColumn, tileRow, tileid = 0;

        x = layerPos.getX() / pTileLayer->getTileSize();
        y = layerPos.getY() / pTileLayer->getTileSize();

        Vector2D startPos = newPos;
        startPos.m_x += 15;
        startPos.m_y += 20;
        Vector2D endPos(newPos.m_x + (m_width - 15), (newPos.m_y) +
        m_height - 4);

        for(int i = startPos.m_x; i < endPos.m_x; i++)
        {
          for(int j = startPos.m_y; j < endPos.m_y; j++)
          {
            tileColumn = i / pTileLayer->getTileSize();
            tileRow = j / pTileLayer->getTileSize();

            tileid = tiles[tileRow + y][tileColumn + x];

            if(tileid != 0)
            {
              return true;
            }
          }
        }
      }

      return false;
    }
}
```

This is quite a large function, but it is essentially the same as how Alien Attack checked for tile collisions. One difference is the y position check:

```
if(newPos.m_y + m_height >= TheGame::Instance()->getGameHeight() - 32)
{
  return false;
}
```

This is used to ensure that we can fall off the map (or fall into a hole) without the function trying to access tiles that are not there. For example, if the object's position is outside the map, the following code would try to access tiles that do not exist and would therefore fail:

```
tileid = tiles[tileRow + y][tileColumn + x];
```

The y value check prevents this.

The Camera class

In a game such as Alien Attack, precise map-collision detection is not terribly important; it is a lot more important to have precise bullet, player, and enemy collisions. A platform game, however, needs very precise map collision requiring the need for a slightly different way of moving the map, so that no precision is lost when scrolling.

In Alien Attack, the map did not actually move; some variables were used to determine which point of the map to draw and this gave the illusion of the map scrolling. In Conan the Caveman, the map will move so that any collision detection routines are relative to the actual position of the map. For this a `Camera` class was created:

```
class Camera
{
public:

  static Camera* Instance()
  {
    if(s_pCamera == 0)
    {
      s_pCamera = new Camera();
    }

    return s_pCamera;
  }
```

```
    void update(Vector2D velocity);

    void setTarget(Vector2D* target) { m_pTarget = target; }
    void setPosition(const Vector2D& position) { m_position =
    position; }

    const Vector2D getPosition() const;


private:

    Camera();
    ~Camera();

    // the camera's target
    Vector2D* m_pTarget;

    // the camera's position
    Vector2D m_position;

    static Camera* s_pCamera;
};

typedef Camera TheCamera;
```

This class is very simple, as it merely holds a location and updates it using the position of a target, referred to the pointer as `m_pTarget`:

```
    const Vector2DCamera::getPosition() const
    {
    {
      if(m_pTarget != 0)
      {
        Vector2D pos(m_pTarget->m_x - (TheGame::Instance()
        ->getGameWidth() / 2), 0);

        if(pos.m_x< 0)
        {
          pos.m_x = 0;
        }

        return pos;
      }

      return m_position;
    }
```

This could also be updated to include the y value as well, but because this is a horizontal-scrolling game, it is not needed here and so the y is returned as 0. This camera position is used to move the map and decide which tiles to draw.

Camera-controlled map

The `TileLayer` class now needs to know the complete size of the map rather than just one section of it; this is passed in through the constructor:

```
TileLayer(int tileSize, int mapWidth, int mapHeight, const
std::vector<Tileset>& tilesets);
```

`LevelParser` passes the height and width in as it creates each `TileLayer`:

```
void LevelParser::parseTileLayer(TiXmlElement* pTileElement,
std::vector<Layer*> *pLayers, const std::vector<Tileset>* pTilesets,
std::vector<TileLayer*> *pCollisionLayers)
{
TileLayer* pTileLayer = new TileLayer(m_tileSize, m_width, m_height,
*pTilesets);
```

The `TileLayer` class uses these values to set its row and column variables:

```
TileLayer::TileLayer(int tileSize, int mapWidth, int mapHeight,
const std::vector<Tileset>& tilesets) : m_tileSize(tileSize), m_
tilesets(tilesets), m_position(0,0), m_velocity(0,0)
{
  m_numColumns = mapWidth;
  m_numRows = mapHeight;

  m_mapWidth = mapWidth;
}
```

With these changes, the tile map now moves according to the position of the camera and skips any tiles that are outside the viewable area:

```
void TileLayer::render()
{
  int x, y, x2, y2 = 0;

  x = m_position.getX() / m_tileSize;
  y = m_position.getY() / m_tileSize;

  x2 = int(m_position.getX()) % m_tileSize;
  y2 = int(m_position.getY()) % m_tileSize;

  for(int i = 0; i < m_numRows; i++)
```

```
  {
    for(int j = 0; j < m_numColumns; j++)
    {
      int id = m_tileIDs[i + y][j + x];

      if(id == 0)
      {
        continue;
      }

      // if outside the viewable area then skip the tile
      if(((j * m_tileSize) - x2) - TheCamera::Instance()
      ->getPosition().m_x < -m_tileSize || ((j * m_tileSize) - x2)
      - TheCamera::Instance()->getPosition()
      .m_x > TheGame::Instance()->getGameWidth())
      {
        continue;
      }

      Tileset tileset = getTilesetByID(id);

      id--;

      // draw the tile into position while offsetting its x
      position by
      // subtracting the camera position
      TheTextureManager::Instance()->drawTile(tileset.name,
      tileset.margin, tileset.spacing, ((j * m_tileSize) - x2) -
      TheCamera::Instance()->getPosition().m_x, ((i * m_tileSize)
      - y2), m_tileSize, m_tileSize, (id - (tileset.firstGridID -
      1)) / tileset.numColumns, (id - (tileset.firstGridID - 1)) %
      tileset.numColumns, TheGame::Instance()->getRenderer());
    }
  }
```

The Player class

The Player class now has to contend with jumping as well as moving, all while checking for map collisions. The Player::update function has undergone quite a change:

```
void Player::update()
{
  if(!m_bDying)
  {
    // fell off the edge
```

```cpp
      if(m_position.m_y + m_height >= 470)
      {
        collision();
      }

      // get the player input
      handleInput();

      if(m_bMoveLeft)
      {
        if(m_bRunning)
        {
          m_velocity.m_x = -5;
        }
        else
        {
          m_velocity.m_x = -2;
        }
      }
      else if(m_bMoveRight)
      {
        if(m_bRunning)
        {
          m_velocity.m_x = 5;
        }
        else
        {
          m_velocity.m_x = 2;
        }
      }
      else
      {
        m_velocity.m_x = 0;
      }

      // if we are higher than the jump height set jumping to false
      if(m_position.m_y < m_lastSafePos.m_y - m_jumpHeight)
      {
        m_bJumping = false;
      }

      if(!m_bJumping)
      {
        m_velocity.m_y = 5;
```

```
      }
      else
      {
        m_velocity.m_y = -5;
      }

      handleMovement(m_velocity);
    }
    else
    {
      m_velocity.m_x = 0;
      if(m_dyingCounter == m_dyingTime)
      {
        ressurect();
      }
      m_dyingCounter++;

      m_velocity.m_y = 5;
    }
    handleAnimation();
}
```

As movement is such an important part of this class, there is a function that is dedicated to handling it:

```
void Player::handleMovement(Vector2D velocity)
{
  // get the current position
  Vector2D newPos = m_position;

  // add velocity to the x position
  newPos.m_x  = m_position.m_x + velocity.m_x;

  // check if the new x position would collide with a tile
  if(!checkCollideTile(newPos))
  {
    // no collision, add to the actual x position
    m_position.m_x = newPos.m_x;
  }
  else
  {
    // collision, stop x movement
    m_velocity.m_x = 0;
  }
```

```cpp
// get the current position after x movement
newPos = m_position;

// add velocity to y position
newPos.m_y += velocity.m_y;

// check if new y position would collide with a tile
if(!checkCollideTile(newPos))
{
  // no collision, add to the actual x position
  m_position.m_y = newPos.m_y;
}
else
{
  // collision, stop y movement
  m_velocity.m_y = 0;

  //  we collided with the map which means we are safe on the ground,
  //  make this the last safe position
  m_lastSafePos = m_position;

  // move the safe pos slightly back or forward so when
  resurrected we are safely on the ground after a fall
  if(velocity.m_x > 0)
  {
    m_lastSafePos.m_x -= 32;
  }
  else if(velocity.m_x < 0)
  {
    m_lastSafePos.m_x += 32;
  }

  // allow the player to jump again
  m_bCanJump = true;

  // jumping is now false
  m_bJumping = false;
}
```

> Notice that x and y checking has been split into two different parts; this is extremely important to make sure that an x collision doesn't stop y movement and vice versa.

The `m_lastSafePos` variable is used to put the player back into a safe spot after they are respawned. For example, if the player was to fall off the edge of the platform in the following screenshot and therefore land on the spikes below, he would be respawned at pretty much the same place as in the screenshot:

Finally, the handle input function now sets Boolean variables for moving to the right-hand side and left-hand side or jumping:

```
void Player::handleInput()
{
  if(TheInputHandler::Instance()->isKeyDown(SDL_SCANCODE_RIGHT) &&
  m_position.m_x < ((*m_pCollisionLayers->begin())->getMapWidth()
  * 32))
  {
    if(TheInputHandler::Instance()->isKeyDown(SDL_SCANCODE_A))
    {
      m_bRunning = true;
    }
    else
    {
      m_bRunning = false;
    }
```

```cpp
      m_bMoveRight = true;
      m_bMoveLeft = false;
    }
    else if(TheInputHandler::Instance()
    ->isKeyDown(SDL_SCANCODE_LEFT) && m_position.m_x > 32)
    {
      if(TheInputHandler::Instance()->isKeyDown(SDL_SCANCODE_A))
      {
        m_bRunning = true;
      }
      else
      {
        m_bRunning = false;
      }

      m_bMoveRight = false;
      m_bMoveLeft = true;
    }
    else
    {
      m_bMoveRight = false;
      m_bMoveLeft = false;
    }

    if(TheInputHandler::Instance()->isKeyDown(SDL_SCANCODE_SPACE)
    && m_bCanJump && !m_bPressedJump)
    {
      TheSoundManager::Instance()->playSound("jump", 0);
      if(!m_bPressedJump)
      {
        m_bJumping = true;
        m_bCanJump = false;
        m_lastSafePos = m_position;
        m_bPressedJump = true;
      }
    }

    if(!TheInputHandler::Instance()->isKeyDown(SDL_SCANCODE_SPACE)
    && m_bCanJump)
    {
      m_bPressedJump = false;
    }
  }
```

This is all fairly self-explanatory apart from the jumping. When the player jumps, it sets the m_bCanJump variable to false, so that on the next loop the jump will not be called again, due to the fact that jump can only happen when the m_bCanJump variable is true; (landing after the jump sets this variable back to true).

Possible additions

It wouldn't be hard to improve on Conan the Caveman's gameplay; increasing enemy and trap numbers would make the game significantly more exciting to play. The game could also benefit from some height to the levels so that players could really explore the map (Metroid style). Other gameplay improvements could include moving platforms, ladders, and bosses.

Summary

Our reusable framework has proved its worth; two games have been created with minimal code duplication.

This chapter looked at scrolling a tile map using the position of the player along with collision detection. Tile-map collision was also covered, along with the important point of splitting x and y movement for effective movement in a platform game. Conan the Caveman is a great starting point for any other 2D game such as a scrolling beat-em-up or even a merging of this chapter and the last to create a platform shooter.

I hope that by now you have a good understanding of how to use SDL2.0 along with C++ to create games and how to effectively break game code apart to create a reusable framework. This is only the start and there are many more game-programming adventures ahead. Good luck!

Index

A

abstract base classes
　using 60
Alien Attack game
　about 191, 192
　additions 192
　basic objects, setting up 196
　bullets, handling 207
　collisions, dealing with 211
　sound SDL_mixer extension, using 193
　tips 216
AnimatedGraphic class 126, 154

B

Base64 decoder 171
base64 encoding 162
basic game objects
　enemy types 204
　GameObject base class 196, 198
　player object 200-204
　scrolling background, adding 205
　SDLGameObject class, renaming to
　　ShooterObject 199, 200
　setting up 196
boolfullscreen parameter 27
Bullet class 218
BulletHandler class 209
bullet handling
　BulletHandler class 209, 210
　scrolling background, adding 207
　types 207, 209

C

C++11 standard 198

Camera class 222, 223
camera-controlled map 224, 225
checkCollideTile function 220
**checkEnemyPlayerBulletCollision
　　functions 214**
checkPlayerEnemyCollision functions 214
clean function 20
CollisionManager Class 214
collisions
　CollisionManager Class, creating 214
　dealing with 211-214
CollisonManager class 218
Conan the Caveman game
　about 217
　additions 231
　basic game objects, setting up 218
　bullet collisions 218
　Camera class 222, 223
　camera-controlled map 224, 225
　game objects 219
　map collisions 219
　Player class 225-231
　screenshot 218
　ShooterObject, renaming as
　　PlatformerObject 219-222

D

Data-driven Design 131
destination rectangle
　about 32-35
　images, flipping 37, 38
　sprite sheet, animating 35, 37
draw function 43, 66, 210

E

Enter key 108
enum attribute 94

F

Finite State Machines. *See* FSM
fixed frames per second. *See* FPS
FPS 77, 78
FSM
  about 103
  game states, base class 103-106
  implementing 103-109

G

game
  code, functioning 20
  Hello SDL code, breaking up 18-20
  structure 17, 18
Game class
  about 21-25, 47
  fullscreen SDL 26, 27
Game::getGameHeight functions 175
Game::getGameWidth 175
Game::handleEvents function 108
Game::init function 84, 108
GameObject class 51
GameObject: class 129
GameObject classes
  altering 138, 139, 140
game objects
  steps, sumarizing 62-67
game objects movement
  acceleration, adding 77
  Cartesian coordinate system 70
  setting up 70
  vector 70, 72
  Vector2D class, adding 75
  velocity, adding 76, 77
game over state
  loading 153, 154
GameOverState class 125, 128
gamepad input 80
Game::setCurrentLevel function 204
GameState.h 103

game states
  about 101
  switching ways 101, 102
getButtonState function 92
getRenderer function 65

H

Hello SDL
  about 13, 14
  initialisation flags 16
  overview 14, 15
  renderer flags 17

I

inheritance
  about 49
  derived classes 61
  functionality example 49-55
  possible performance penalties 62
  result tips 61
  using 61
init function 23
initialisation flags, SDL
  about 16
  SDL_INIT_AUDIO 16
  SDL_INIT_EVERYTHING 16
  SDL_INIT_HAPTIC 16
  SDL_INIT_JOYSTICK 16
  SDL_INIT_NOPARACHUTE 16
  SDL_INIT_TIMER 16
  SDL_INIT_VIDEO 16
input handling
  about 79
  axis movement, handling 84-90
  input handler class, creating 79
  joystick 80
  joystick button input, dealing with 91-93
  mouse events, handling 93
  summary 98, 99
Instance function 46
int flags parameter 27

J

joy parameter 85
joystick button input 91

Joystick Control Panel property 80
joysticks
  events 80
  initializing 81-84

L

Level class 166
LevelParser class
  creating 168-170
LevelParser::parseLevel 212
load function 154, 195

M

MainMenuState class 148, 150
m_bCanJump variable 231
MenuButton class 147
MenuState.cpp file 104
menu states
  callback functions 114, 116
  fuction parameters 114
  game over state, creating 123-129
  implementing 110-114
  temporary play state,
    implementing 117-123
m_lastSafePos variable 229
mouse events
  button events, handling 93-95
  handling 93
  keyboard input, implementing 96, 97
  motion events, handling 95, 96

N

non-player character. *See* **NPC**
NPC 49

O

Object Factories
  about 134, 135
  Distributed Factories, using 135-138
Object Layer 182
object layers
  ObjectLayer class, developing 184-188
  parsing 182, 183

object-oriented programming. *See* **OOP**
onEnter function 107, 127, 154
onExit function 107
OOP 49

P

parseLevel function 168, 185
parseObjects function 145, 146, 186
pause state
  loading 152, 153
PauseState.cpp file 121
Player class 225-231
Player::update function 90, 225
Player::update function 204
playSound or playMusic functions 196
play state
  loading 150, 151
PlayState class 123
polymorphism
  about 55
  implementing 55-60
pState parameter 107

Q

Quadtree 216
quit function 83

R

registerType function 136
renderer flags, SDL
  SDL_RENDERER_ACCELERATED 17
  SDL_RENDERER_PRESENTVSYNC 17
  SDL_RENDERER_SOFTWARE 17
  SDL_RENDERER_TARGETTEXTURE 17
render function 102, 180
Rich Text Format. *See* **RTF**
RTF 7

S

ScrollingBackground class 205
SDL
  about 5
  drawing 29
  need for 6

SDL 1.2
  extensions 7
SDL 1.2 extensions
  about 7
  SDL_image 7
  SDL_mixer 7
  SDL_net 7
  SDL_rtf 7
  SDL_ttf 7
SDL 2.0
  about 6, 7
  SDL 1.2 extensions 7
SDL 2.0 Roadmap 6
SDL_CreateRenderer function 14
SDL_CreateWindow function 27
SDL drawing
  about 29
  images, obtaining 29
  texture, creating 30, 31
SDL_image
  installing 38-40
  using 40, 41
SDL_INIT_AUDIO flag 16
SDL_INIT_EVERYTHING flag 16
SDL_INIT_HAPTIC flag 16
SDL_INIT_JOYSTICK flag 16
SDL_INIT_NOPARACHUTE flag 16
SDL_INIT_TIMER flag 16
SDL_INIT_VIDEO flag 16
SDL_JOYAXISMOTION event 88
SDL_JoyBallEvent 80
SDL_JoyButtonEvent 80
SDL_JoyHatEvent 80
SDL joystick events
  about 80, 81
  SDL_JoyAxisEvent 80
  SDL_JoyBallEvent 80
  SDL_JoyButtonEvent 80
  SDL_JoyHatEvent 80
SDL_MouseButtonEvent 93
SDL Mouse Event
  SDL_MouseButtonEvent 93
  SDL_MouseMotionEvent 93
  SDL_MouseWheelEvent 93
SDL_MouseMotionEvent 93
SDL_MouseWheelEvent 93
SDL_RENDERER_ACCELERATED flag 17

SDL_RendererFlip value
  SDL_FLIP_HORIZONTAL 38
  SDL_FLIP_NONE 38
  SDL_FLIP_VERTICAL 38
SDL_RENDERER_PRESENTVSYNC
    flag 17
SDL_RENDERER_SOFTWARE flag 17
SDL_RENDERER_TARGETTEXTURE
    flag 17
SDL setup, in Visual C++ Express 2010
  about 8
  library, retrieving 8
  linking 10-12
  Mercurial, using 8
  SDL 2.0 repository, building 8-10
  SDL 2.0 repository, cloning 8, 10
SDL_WasInit() function 16
SDL_WINDOW_BORDERLESS
    function 26
SDL_WindowFlags function 26
SDL_WindowFlags functions
  SDL_WINDOW_BORDERLESS 26
  SDL_WINDOW_FOREIGN 26
  SDL_WINDOW_FULLSCREEN 26
  SDL_WINDOW_HIDDEN 26
  SDL_WINDOW_INPUT_FOCUS 26
  SDL_WINDOW_INPUT_GRABBED 26
  SDL_WINDOW_MAXIMIZED 26
  SDL_WINDOW_MINIMIZED 26
  SDL_WINDOW_MOUSE_FOCUS 26
  SDL_WINDOW_OPENGL 26
  SDL_WINDOW_RESIZABLE 26
  SDL_WINDOW_SHOWN 26
SDL_WINDOW_FOREIGN function 26
SDL_WINDOW_FULLSCREEN flag 27
SDL_WINDOW_FULLSCREEN function 26
SDL_WINDOW_HIDDEN function 26
SDL_WINDOW_INPUT_FOCUS
    function 26
SDL_WINDOW_INPUT_GRABBED
    function 26
SDL_WINDOW_MAXIMIZED function 26
SDL_WINDOW_MINIMIZED function 26
SDL_WINDOW_MOUSE_FOCUS
    function 26
SDL_WINDOW_OPENGL function 26
SDL_WINDOW_RESIZABLE function 26

SDL_WINDOW_SHOWN function 26
setCallbacks function 152
Simple DirectMedia Layer. *See* SDL
SoundManager class 196
sound SDL_mixer extension
  SoundManager class, creating 193-196
  using 193
source rectangle
  about 32-35
  images, flipping 37, 38
  sprite sheet, animating 35, 37
states, XML file
  game over state, loading 153, 154
  menu state, loading 147-149
  parsing 140-146
  pause state, loading 152, 153
  play state, loading 150, 151

T

texture manager
  about 42
  creating 42-45
  using, as singleton 46
TextureManager class 42
Tiled application 160-164
tiled map editor 157
tile layer
  parsing 171-174
TileLayer class 224
TileLayer update function 175
tile map
  about 157-159
  drawing 165, 175-180
  LevelParser class, creating 168-170
  parsing 165, 166
  scrolling 180, 181
  TileLayer class, creating 167

tile layer, parsing 171-174
tilesets, parsing 170, 171
tilesets
  parsing 170, 171
TortoiseHg Workbench window 8
type function 214

U

uncompress function 174
update function 45, 116, 129, 210

V

vector
  about 70
  multiplying, by scalar number 73
  normalizing 74
  sclar number, dividing by 74
  substration methods 73
  two vectors, adding 72
  using 71
Visual C++ Express 2010
  SDL, setting up 8

X

Xbox 360 controller 81
XML file
  about 131, 132
  basic XML structure 132-134
  menu state, loading 147-149
  other states, loading 150
  states, parsing 140-147

Z

zlib compression algorithm 162

[PACKT PUBLISHING] Thank you for buying
SDL Game Development

About Packt Publishing

Packt, pronounced 'packed', published its first book "*Mastering phpMyAdmin for Effective MySQL Management*" in April 2004 and subsequently continued to specialize in publishing highly focused books on specific technologies and solutions.

Our books and publications share the experiences of your fellow IT professionals in adapting and customizing today's systems, applications, and frameworks. Our solution based books give you the knowledge and power to customize the software and technologies you're using to get the job done. Packt books are more specific and less general than the IT books you have seen in the past. Our unique business model allows us to bring you more focused information, giving you more of what you need to know, and less of what you don't.

Packt is a modern, yet unique publishing company, which focuses on producing quality, cutting-edge books for communities of developers, administrators, and newbies alike. For more information, please visit our website: www.packtpub.com.

Writing for Packt

We welcome all inquiries from people who are interested in authoring. Book proposals should be sent to author@packtpub.com. If your book idea is still at an early stage and you would like to discuss it first before writing a formal book proposal, contact us; one of our commissioning editors will get in touch with you.

We're not just looking for published authors; if you have strong technical skills but no writing experience, our experienced editors can help you develop a writing career, or simply get some additional reward for your expertise.

Torque 3D Game Development Cookbook

ISBN: 978-1-84969-354-7   Paperback: 380 pages

Over 80 practical recipes and hidden gems for getting the most out of the Torque 3D game engine

1. Clear step-by-step instruction and practical examples to advance your understanding of Torque 3D and all of its sub-systems

2. Explore essential topics such as graphics, sound, networking and user input

3. Helpful tips and techniques to increase the potential of your Torque 3D games

jQuery Game Development Essentials

ISBN: 978-1-84969-506-0   Paperback: 244 pages

Learn how to make fun and addictive multi-platform games using jQuery

1. Discover how you can create a fantastic RPG, arcade game, or platformer using jQuery!

2. Learn how you can integrate your game with various social networks, creating multiplayer experiences and also ensuring compatibility with mobile devices.

3. Create your very own framework, harnessing the very best design patterns and proven techniques along the way.

Please check **www.PacktPub.com** for information on our titles